Advance Praise for

THE SUSTAINABILITY REVOLUTION

The Sustainability Revolution is a compelling reminder of the power each of us has to make this world a better place through our everyday actions. Indeed, if we are to survive we must recognize our place in the natural world and make a concerted effort to leave lighter ecological footprints. *The Sustainability Revolution* shines light on the path that we all must follow to make this world a more sustainable and peaceful place for all living things.

— DR. JANE GOODALL, DBE
Founder – the Jane Goodall Institute
UN Messenger of Peace

Andrés Edwards maps one of the most significant yet least understood landscapes: the landscape with the paths to the place where all people can flourish, within the means of one generous, but ultimately limited planet. His map brings clarity to the formerly confusing mountains and valleys of sustainability principles, ideas, concepts, and indicators. I wish this book becomes everybody's "Rand McNally Atlas" to guide us on the rally to sustainability. This is the best rally since we can all win. Andrés' brilliant book shows us how.

— MATHIS WACKERNAGEL, Executive Director,
Global Footprint Network

Like a father penciling his kid's height marks on a door jamb, Andrés Edwards has lovingly taken the measure of the sustainability movement's leaps-and-bounds growth. Seeing our collective wisdom arrayed in a single book is powerful medicine for long-time solution seekers, and an irresistible invitation to a new generation wondering, "how shall we live here?"

JANINE BENYUS, author of *Biomimicry: Innovation Inspired By Nature*
and cofounder, Biomimicry Guild.

In *The Sustainability Revolution*, Andrés Edwards collects a comprehensive set of sustainability principles into the definitive desk reference. The principles are complemented with an excellent overview of social movements and the evolution from environmentalism to sustainability. This book is a fundamental tool for those building a better world — a must for your library!

— RANDY HAYES, founder of Rainforest Action Network, director of sustainability for the City of Oakland

Andrés Edwards has done society a great service with *The Sustainability Revolution*. He has helped us envision a sustainable world by illuminating the thousands of positive efforts worldwide. The book is both an inspiration and a testimony — it is a much-needed shot in the arm for the sustainability movement.

— ANTHONY D. CORTESE, president of Second Nature, leader in the Education for Sustainability movement in higher education

Andrés Edwards has written a comprehensive guidebook to the Sustainability Movement, its history, principles, and applications. At a time when so many people feel the bad guys are winning, Edwards shows us the quiet good news that doesn't get headlines. We and the planet have a chance, and *The Sustainability Revolution* shows why and how.

— SIM VAN DER RYN, architect, author of *Ecological Design* and *Design For Life*

What is ecological sustainability, and is it one consistent thing? And can we protect the children of the future and still make a good living today? Andrés Edwards has given us an elegant and concise way to say 'Yes!' to both questions. He shows just how coherent is the worldview of the sustainability movement, and that its principles and practices are moving steadily from grand ideas, and statements of alarm, toward actual, everyday practicality. It's not just that "a better world is possible." It's happening. It's real.

— PAUL H. RAY, co-author of *The Cultural Creatives*

Sustainability is more than a buzzword; it is a concept that defines what is needed for our civilization to survive. The discussion about sustainability is therefore the most important one now occurring on the planet. Andrés Edwards has summarized the current state of this discussion in a thorough, upbeat, and understandable way. *The Sustainability Revolution* highlights not only the ideas, but the courageous efforts of people around the world who are creating a way of life that is not only more survivable, but more just and satisfying as well.

— RICHARD HEINBERG, professor of human ecology,
New College of California, and author of *The Party's Over: Oil, War and the Fate of Industrial Societies* and *Powerdown: Options and Actions for a Post-Carbon World*

The Sustainability Revolution presents a clear, concise, straightforward articulation of the most powerful force sweeping the world. This book is a great source of inspiration, showing us just how much is going on behind the scenes all over the world

— SPENCER B. BEEBE, founder, Ecotrust

By the simple act of gathering in one place dozens of lists of "sustainability principles," Andrés Edwards has sketched the landscape — and given us a glimpse of the trajectory — of the sustainability revolution.

— GIL FRIEND, president & CEO, Natural Logic Inc.,
and author of *A Declaration of Leadership*

The Sustainability Revolution provides a brilliant synthesis of the multiple braids of sustainability. Its comprehensive analysis of sustainability principles and frameworks is particularly valuable.

— STUART COWAN, co-author of *Ecological Design*

In this immensely useful book, Edwards provides an impressive guide to the future by examining the pathbreaking actions and innovative ideas already moving forward in the world. *The Sustainability Revolution* is at once practical and visionary.

— JAMES GUSTAVE SPETH, Dean, Yale School of Forestry
and Environmental Studies

THE

SUSTAINABILITY
REVOLUTION

portrait of a paradigm shift

ANDRES R. EDWARDS

foreword by David W. Orr

NEW SOCIETY PUBLISHERS

Cataloging in Publication Data
A catalog record for this publication is available from the National Library of Canada.

Copyright © 2005 by Andrés Edwards.
All rights reserved.

Cover design by Diane McIntosh. Leaf image ©Photodisc Blue.

Printed in Canada. Third printing December 2006.

Paperback ISBN-10: 0-86571-531-9
Paperback ISBN-13: 978-0-86571-531-8

Inquiries regarding requests to reprint all or part of *The Sustainability Revolution* should be addressed to New Society Publishers at the address below.

To order directly from the publishers, please call toll-free (North America) 1-800-567-6772, or order online at www.newsociety.com

Any other inquiries can be directed by mail to:

New Society Publishers
P.O. Box 189, Gabriola Island, BC V0R 1X0, Canada
1-800-567-6772

New Society Publishers' mission is to publish books that contribute in fundamental ways to building an ecologically sustainable and just society, and to do so with the least possible impact on the environment, in a manner that models this vision. We are committed to doing this not just through education, but through action. We are acting on our commitment to the world's remaining ancient forests by phasing out our paper supply from ancient forests worldwide. This book is one step toward ending global deforestation and climate change. It is printed on acid-free paper that is 100% old growth forest-free (100% post-consumer recycled), processed chlorine free, and printed with vegetable based, low VOC inks. For further information, or to browse our full list of books and purchase securely, visit our website at: www.newsociety.com

NEW SOCIETY PUBLISHERS   www.newsociety.com

Contents

To Rochelle, Naomi, Easton and Rylan

Acknowledgments

T HIS BOOK GREW from a synthesis of lively discussions exploring sustainability concepts during seminars at New College of California and with numerous other colleagues and friends over the years. I would like to thank David Caploe for his vision, perseverance and guidance, which were instrumental to the development of this effort. Tam Beeler's humor and wise counsel helped me keep the "big picture" in mind. Mutombo Mpanya's and Ann Hancock's uncommon insights also were of great assistance, particularly during the conceptual phase of this work.

The refreshing perspectives from the "Design Team" — Beth Meredith, Martha Glessing, and Nobu Sakamoto — in developing tangible projects that highlight sustainability concepts provided a foundation for exploring the subjects discussed in this book.

I am grateful to Bob Apte for his friendship, creativity and shared ecological and cultural interests, which have enriched my outlook on the topics covered herein. I wish to thank David Orr for writing the foreword and for his pioneering work in ecoliteracy and sustainability education.

I appreciate the suggestions of Steve Beck, Nick Brown, Susan Burns, Fritjof Capra, Stuart Cowan, Adam Davis, John Garn, Bruce Hammond, Richard Heinberg, Charles McGlashan, Carol Misseldine, Steve Piersanti, Jean Rogers, Ruth Rominger, Sam Ruark, Mark Samolis, David Schaller, Rand Selig and Sissel Waage, who have contributed to the ideas explored in this book. I also wish to acknowledge all those who reviewed the manuscript and offered their feedback.

I would like to thank Debra Amador and Linda Steck for reviewing sections of the manuscript, and Chris Plant, Judith Plant, Heather Wardle and their team at New Society Publishers for their vision and creativity. I greatly appreciate the work and dedication of Ingrid Witvoet and Diane Killou for their editing and expertise in shaping the text and graphic layout to their final form.

Finally, I wish to express my deep gratitude to my wife, Rochelle, and my children, Naomi, Easton and Rylan, who are a wellspring of inspiration.

By David W. Orr

A T THE END OF HIS LIFE, SCIENCE-FICTION WRITER and historian H. G. Wells was no optimist. Surveying things from his vantage point at the close of World War II and not long before his own death he wrote: "The end of everything we call life is close at hand and cannot be evaded" (H. G. Wells, 1946, p. 1). And 58 years later, Martin Rees, England's Astronomer Royal and professor at Cambridge University, was no more optimistic, giving humankind 50-50 odds of making it to the year 2100 (Rees, 2003, p. 8). Indeed, any moderately well-informed high-school student could easily assemble a list of dozens of ways things could all come undone, ranging from whimpers to bangs. Gamblers at some intergalactic casino would not likely bet much on us. And what can be said for such a violent bunch that seems so intent on mutilating its own earthly home? We are a long shot, but so, too, were those small, unimpressive mammals scurrying about amidst the invincible dinosaurs of their time. If such intergalactic bets *are* being placed, there are a perceptive few who might see a modern-day equivalent to that earlier time when the long shot paid off. The small, vulnerable and unimpressive mammals won for many reasons, including their agility, resilience, adaptability and intelligence-to-body-mass ratio.

All informed citizens know about the perils ahead, including rapid climate destabilization, species extinction, pollution, terrorism and ecological unraveling in its many forms, and the human, political and economic consequences. But fewer have stopped to look at the wider topography, where something quite remarkable is occurring. Below the radar screen and outside the cultural buzz, a revolution is beginning to gather steam at the grassroots and in out-of-the-way places around the world. While the headlines report one military excursion or another on the chessboard of geopolitics, or yet another "triumph" for the juggernaut of globalization, people and small organizations with long names and short budgets are beginning to construct a different world. As unimpressive as those small furry mammals were relative to the giants of a distant time, the outline of something far better is beginning to emerge in communities and organizations around the world.

It is happening first at the periphery of power and wealth, where revolutions often start. It is evident in farmers beginning to mimic natural systems in order to preserve their soil and land. It is evident in a new attitude emerging everywhere about the value of biological diversity and species protection. It is evident in the rapid development of technologies that harness sunlight and wind. It is evident in the burgeoning interest in green building, green architecture, green engineering and green communities. It is evident in a growing number of businesses selling "products of service" and preserving natural capital as a matter of conscience and profit. It is evident in a new religious sensibility across the full spectrum of faith traditions that regards stewardship of the Earth as obligatory. It is evident in education and the emergence of new ways to think about the human role in nature that stretch our perspective to whole systems and out to the far horizon of imagination.

The "it" is often called "sustainability," an indefinite term. But by whatever name, this revolution is more sweeping by far than that which we associate with the Enlightenment of the 18th century. The sustainability revolution is nothing less than a rethinking and remaking of our role in the natural world. It is a recalibration of human intentions to coincide with the way the biophysical world works. It is a slowing down to the rhythms of our bodies, convivial association and nature. The concern for our longevity as a species represents a maturing of our kind to consider ourselves first as "plain members and citizens" of an ecological community, and second as trustees of all that is past with all that is yet to come — a mystic chain of gratitude, obligation, compassion and hope.

If this revolution grows and matures as I believe that it will, it will do one other thing: it will improve our worthiness to be sustained. Imagine a tribunal of all species sitting in judgment over Homo sapiens charged to rule on our fitness to remain on Earth based on our behavior over the past ten thousand years. How would we be judged? Other than the votes of cockroaches, crows and any number of viruses, the motion to evict us would win by a large margin. Even to raise the question, however, would be taken as a sign of misanthropy or worse. But failure to do so rests on the fatal assumption that we live outside the community of life and beyond the call to a larger duty than that of human dominion. The revolution described here, in other words, is not simply about making ourselves physically sustainable at whatever cost, but rather about something akin to a species maturing into its fullest stature — one worthy of being sustained — a revolution of charity, magnanimity and spirit.

In the pages that follow, educator, designer and consultant Andrés Edwards paints what he calls a portrait of this revolution. His description crosses national boundaries as well as the divisions between academic disciplines and sectors of the economy. The sustainability revolution is steadily reshaping our lives and our place in the larger fabric of life for the better. But there is nothing inevitable about any revolution or about any good thing. Ultimately these are matters of choice and fate. But this book helps us put the odds in perspective and clarify the point that despair can be overcome by a revolution of hope, competence and intelligence underlain by wisdom.

[David W. Orr is Paul Sears Distinguished Professor, Oberlin College, and is the author of *Ecological Literacy, Earth in Mind, The Nature of Design*, and *The Last Refuge*.]

Portrait of the Sustainability Revolution

Every generation needs a new revolution.
—Thomas Jefferson

We must not be afraid of dreaming the seemingly impossible if we want the seemingly impossible to become a reality.
—Vaclav Havel

IN BORNEO, villagers are replacing polluting diesel generators with small-scale hydro-generators and tapping local streams to produce clean and affordable electricity for their communities.[1] In Astoria, Oregon, local government, businesses and residents have used ecological design practices to transform an abandoned toxic mill site into a convivial community.[2] In Bavaria, Germany, the world's largest solar power plant, a 30-acre facility generating 10 megawatts of electricity — enough to meet the demand of 9,000 German homes — is online.[3] And in Curitiba, Brazil, city planners have created a model public transportation system covering eight neighboring cities and carrying 1.9 million passengers a day.[4] Although these events may appear to be isolated incidents, they represent thousands of initiatives taking place worldwide that are the vanguard of the Sustainability Revolution.

Not since the Industrial Revolution of the mid-18th to mid-19th centuries has such a profound transformation with worldwide impact emerged onto the world stage. Like its industrial counterpart, the Sustainability Revolution is creating a pervasive and permanent shift in consciousness and worldview affecting all facets of society.

The Sustainability Revolution draws its significance and global impact from a wide spectrum of interests with common fundamental values. Like the Industrial Revolution, the Sustainability Revolution is far-reaching and is having a profound impact, shaping everything from the places we live and work to the foods we eat and the endeavors we pursue as individuals and as communities.

Though still largely underground and misunderstood, the Sustainability Revolution is affecting the economic, ecological and social aspects of societies worldwide. Amid the invasion of SUVs, Costcos, Wal-Marts and supermarket chains, we see glimpses of this transformation in the increasing numbers of hybrid cars, wind turbines and solar panel installations; the resurgence of farmers' markets and organic foods in cities and towns across Europe and the US; the introduction of ecoliteracy curricula in some schools and universities; the building of cohousing projects that restore community ties; and the large number of grass-roots groups from around the world working on issues such as habitat restoration, climate change, labor rights, local currencies and the protection of local economies. These changes, though inconspicuous, are blazing a trail toward a new awareness that treats the fabric of life of our planet with respect and seeks to balance economic goals and ecological health.

The present unsustainable path marked by an unrelenting economy that methodically depletes the Earth's ecosystems will have to change. In 2003, for example, 11,000 cars were added to China's roads every day, a total of 4 million new cars in one year. At this pace, by 2015, 150 million cars are expected in China — 18 million more than were driven in the United States in 1999.[5] As Lester Brown points out, if Chinese car ownership and oil consumption were to equal US rates, 80 million barrels of oil a day above current world production would be needed; and if Chinese per-person paper consumption were to match the US level there would not be enough paper (or forests) available.[6]

Clearly the Chinese, together with the rest of the over six billion people in the world, face a predicament that calls for a significant ecological, economic and social shift. The Sustainability Revolution presents an alternative that supports economic viability and healthy ecosystems by modifying consumption patterns and implementing a more equitable social framework.

> ▼
>
> **The Sustainability Revolution presents an alternative that supports economic viability and healthy ecosystems by modifying consumption patterns and implementing a more equitable social framework.**
>
> ▲

Anatomy of Social Revolutions

To better understand the structure of the Sustainability Revolution, we turn to the anatomy of social revolutions. From 1750-1850 the Industrial Revolution caused a lasting shift from an agricultural and commercial society relying on animals and simple tools to an industrial society based on machinery and factories. The Industrial Revolution was marked by technological innovations, increased production capacity and economic specialization. As with other social revolutions, the changes in the Industrial Revolution and the current Sustainability Revolution involve three distinct phases: genesis, critical mass and diffusion.

Genesis

The genesis of the Industrial Revolution was in the accumulation of precious metals brought back to Europe from the New World. These commodities stimulated the creation of industry, expanded trade and established a money economy in Great Britain. The Sustainability Revolution dates back to the concepts first explored in 1972 at the United Nations Conference on the Human

Environment in Stockholm, Sweden, and gained prominence in the 1987 Brundtland report, *Our Common Future.*

The Brundtland report created a framework for addressing ways of protecting the Earth's ecosystems while taking into consideration economic and social justice concerns. Sustainable development was defined as "development that meets the needs of the present without compromising the ability of future generations to meet their own needs."[7]

Critical mass

The critical mass phase of the Industrial Revolution involved the use of power resulting from the improvement of the steam engine by James Watt in 1769. This development had a profound impact on the efficiency of factory production, transportation services and the economic infrastructure of nation states. Although the Sustainability Revolution's critical mass has yet to fully materialize, key milestones were the 1992 Earth Summit in Rio de Janeiro, Brazil, and the development of the personal computer and the Internet.

The Rio summit brought together 182 world leaders and propelled sustainability onto the international stage. Through the Rio Declaration and Agenda 21, the summit developed frameworks for charting future actions. The personal computer and the Internet have had a significant impact on the Sustainability Revolution by facilitating the dissemination of information and the organization of sustainability-oriented groups, which now have better access to media outlets traditionally controlled by well-established institutions.

Diffusion

Although the Industrial Revolution began in Great Britain, it spread throughout Europe and then to the United States and beyond. The use of electricity, the gasoline engine and factory-based production methods was rapidly adopted by other cultures. These changes resulted in urban centers that today are found worldwide.

The Sustainability Revolution emerged in the United States and European Union countries as they grappled with the limits of natural resources and is quickly spreading to developing nations, though it has yet to become a pervasive mainstream phenomenon. Some of the most innovative projects in areas such as renewable energy, agriculture and finance are taking place in the developing nations. One example is a national biogas program in Thailand that converts animal waste into methane for electricity production.[8] Another project is the Grameen Bank in Bangladesh, which in 1976 through collateral-free loans to the very poor sparked the microcredit movement, which has spread to over 40 countries and proven to be a successful anti-poverty program for developing nations and for the inner cities of industrialized countries.[9]

In addition to such initiatives, there now is worldwide awareness of issues such as climate change, pollution, ozone depletion and habitat destruction that are international in scope and will require a concerted effort by all nations to resolve.

Movements and Revolutions

Whereas movements tend to have narrower objectives and are led by a charismatic leader, such as Mahatma Gandhi in the non-violence movement and Martin Luther King in the civil rights movement, social revolutions have wider objectives and are led by a large and diverse number of individuals. The anti-globalization, organic foods, green building, renewable energy and other "green" movements all are working within the broader context of the Sustainability Revolution. Though including aspects of social movements, sustainability is in fact a revolution with a new value system, consciousness and worldview.

The Industrial Revolution was defined by technological breakthroughs including James Watt's improved steam engine (1769), Edward Cartwright's power loom (1783) and Eli Whitney's cotton gin (1793). These inventions contributed to increased production and economic growth in the textile, iron, rail and steamship industries that have left an indelible mark on our current society. The impact of the Industrial Revolution has been broad and lasting.

The developments that have shaped the Sustainability Revolution have transformed the fields of communications (computers, the Internet, e-mail, wireless phones, digital cameras); finance (global trade, international stock and commodities markets); transportation (hybrid cars, overnight parcel delivery, lower-fare jet travel); building (green building, renewable materials, solar energy); and medicine (imaging technology, human genome decoding, cloning); and led to the organization of citizens' groups working on causes such as stream restoration, pesticide control, renewable energy and organic produce.

▼

Although sustainability often is marked by environmental causes and protest campaigns, its values represent a broad context of issues that have spread underground in all sectors of society throughout the world.

▲

The Sustainability Revolution evolved as a reaction to the Industrial Revolution's degradation of the environment and our well-being. The rampant environmental impacts and the recognition of the limits of natural resources combined to produce a new ethos embodied in the Sustainability Revolution. Government environmental clean-up programs such as Superfund and protection programs such as the Clean Air Act, Clean Water Act, Safe Drinking Water Act and Endangered Species Act were created as a result of concern for the damaging effects of the Industrial Revolution.

The Five Characteristics of the Sustainability Revolution

The Sustainability Revolution has five key characteristics or dimensions. These are: (1) remarkable similarities among sustainability groups in overall intentions and objectives; (2) a large and diverse number of such groups; (3) a wide range of issues addressed by these groups; (4) leadership by a group of decentralized visionaries rather than a single charismatic figurehead; and (5) varying modes of action: oppositional and alternative.

Similar Intentions and Objectives

The mainstream often confuses sustainability with ecological concerns, pitting conservation groups against business interests. This situation leads to a deadlock, with polarized viewpoints and inability to compromise. Sustainability has thus been framed in a narrow perspective, often associated with a single issue backed by proponents with a liberal mindset. Although sustainability often is marked by environmental causes and protest campaigns, its values represent a broad context of issues that have spread underground in all sectors of society throughout the world.

Although there are some disagreements among sustainability groups, there are remarkable similarities in their intentions and objectives. These include: concern for the environment, the economy and social equity; understanding of our dependence on the health of natural systems (clean air, clean water, healthy soils and forests, biodiversity) for our survival and well-being; knowledge of the limits of the Earth's ecosystems and the detrimental impact of unchecked human activities (population, pollution, economic growth); and a long-term, intergenerational perspective in actions and goals.

Large and diverse

The Sustainability Revolution is international in scope. Its ideas are promoted by environmental and social service groups, nongovernmental organizations, foundations and loosely organized community groups. All facets of society, including government, industry, the private sector, education and the arts, and all socioeconomic backgrounds, nationalities, religions and cultural affiliations are represented.

Paul Hawken estimates that there are 30,000 sustainability groups in the US and tens of thousands of groups worldwide.[10] Social researcher Paul Ray describes sustainability advocates as "Cultural Creatives" and estimates there are 50 million in the US and 80 to 90 million in the European Union, with a $230 billion market in the US and $500 billion worldwide.[11]

Range of issues

The Sustainability Revolution has no single ideology but instead a collection of values centered around healthy ecosystems, economic viability and social justice. Sustainability encompasses a wide array of issues including: conservation, globalization, socially responsible investing, corporate reform, ecoliteracy, climate change, human rights, population growth, health, biodiversity, labor rights, social and environmental justice, local currency, conflict resolution, women's rights, public policy, trade and organic farming. These issues cross national boundaries, socioeconomic sectors and political systems, touching every facet of society and driven by life-affirming values that influence policies and initiatives at the local, regional, national and international levels.

Decentralized leadership

As with other social revolutions, the leadership in the Sustainability Revolution is made up of hundreds of thousands of citizens and community leaders from around the world. As Hawken reminds us, "No one started this worldview, no one is in charge of it, no orthodoxy is restraining it .... [It is] unrecognizable to the American media because it is not centralized, based on power, or led by charismatic white males."[12]

The strength of the Sustainability Revolution lies in its decentralized, nonhierarchical organizational pattern, which encourages diversity and alternative approaches to the ecological, economic and social challenges of our time. The Sustainability Revolution has spread remarkably quickly and effectively into cultures worldwide.

Oppositional and alternative actions

While some sustainability groups oppose trends seen as detrimental to their core values, others present alternative models. Oppositional actions focus on areas such as globalization, biotechnology and habitat destruction, while alternative actions include voluntary simplicity, supporting local economies and community-building.

The oppositional component of the Sustainability Revolution is increasingly visible through demonstrations at conferences such as the G-8 Summit in Genoa, Italy (2001), the World Trade Organization (WTO) in Seattle, Washington (1999) and Cancun, Mexico (2003) and the Free Trade Area of the Americas (FTAA) in Quebec, Canada (2001) and Miami, Florida (2003).

Nevertheless, important shifts are occurring in a much less dramatic fashion through alternative approaches ranging from local renewable energy projects to Community Supported Agriculture (CSA) programs to corporate initiatives implementing sustainable frameworks such as The Natural Step, which provides a scientifically based organizational model.[13] At the international level, in 2004 the World Social Forum attracted over 80,000 social activists from 132 countries to Mumbai, India, to discuss issues from globalization to patriarchy, militarism and racism, challenging participants: "Another World is Possible! Let's Build It."[14]

A Revolution of Interconnections

The Sustainability Revolution provides a vital new approach to tackling the issues confronting the world today. By taking a comprehensive look at the interconnections among ecological, economic and equity issues ranging from global warming to pollution, health and poverty, we are more likely to seek and implement lasting solutions.

The Sustainability Revolution marks the emergence of a new social ethos emphasizing the web of relationships that link the challenges we currently face. As Carolyn Merchant points out, "An ecological transformation in the deepest sense entails changes in ecology, production, reproduction, and forms of consciousness .... In the ecological model, humans are neither helpless victims nor arrogant dominators of nature, but active participants in the destiny of the webs of which they are a part."[15]

By understanding the characteristics and intentions of the Sustainability Revolution, we will be better prepared to tackle complex problems requiring an open-minded and cooperative approach.

CHAPTER 1

The Birth of Sustainability

As to methods there may be a million and then some,
but principles are few. The man who grasps principles can
successfully select his own methods. The man who tries
methods, ignoring principles, is sure to have trouble.
                                        —Ralph Waldo Emerson

Small shifts in deeply held beliefs and values can massively
alter societal behavior and results — in fact, may be the only
things that ever have.
                                        —Dee Hock

The Context

AT THE DAWN OF THE 21ST CENTURY, a new revolution is gaining strength — the Sustainability Revolution. The purpose of this work is to help those inside this revolution, as well as those presently outside, better understand where sustainability is coming from and where it might be going.

We will begin with a "pre-history" of the Sustainability Revolution, paying special attention to its relationship with its main precursor, the environmental movement of the 1960s and 1970s. Next we will follow the emergence of the Sustainability Revolution in the 1980s and its extraordinary flowering beginning in the 1990s. Then we will examine the reasons for the methodology we will use to grasp the revolution's profound and fruitful diversity. We then will be in a

position to create a multidimensional portrait of the Sustainability
Revolution today.

Environmentalism: The Precursor
to Modern Sustainability

At the foundation of modern sustainability lies the human connection with nature, expressed first in America through the New
England transcendentalist movement of the 1800s. Transcendentalists
such as Bronson Alcott, Margaret Fuller, George Ripley — and especially Henry David Thoreau and Ralph Waldo Emerson — pointed to
the significance of nature as a mystery full of symbols and spirituality.

As Emerson stated, "The Transcendentalist adopts the whole
connection of spiritual doctrine. He believes in miracle, in the perpetual openness of the human mind to new influx of light and
power; he believes in inspiration, and in ecstasy."[1]

In his book *Nature* (1836), Emerson viewed the natural world as
a source of guidance and a mirror that reflects back the soul. He
described our relationship with nature as having seven facets: commodity, beauty, language, discipline, idealism, spirits and prospects.[2]
Each of these facets, in turn, supports the intuition and inspiration
of the individual.

Emerson's description of the natural world as a mirror was
enhanced by the work of his friend and contemporary, Thoreau. In
Walden (1854), Thoreau described his experience of living a simple
existence in a hut next to Walden Pond near Concord, Massachusetts.
Thoreau's observations of nature highlight the virtues of libertarian-
ism and individualism. As he stated, "I went to the woods because I
wished to live deliberately, to front only the essential facts of life, and
see if I could not learn what it had to teach, and not, when I came
to die, discover that I had not lived."[3]

The works of Thoreau and Emerson helped establish the transcendentalist movement's view of nature as a teacher, which was enhanced
by other writers and naturalists in the 20th century. One of these
was the early 20th century American inventor, writer, naturalist and

conservationist John Muir, who played a pivotal role in bringing attention to the importance of preserving America's wildlands.

Unlike the transcendentalists — who saw nature as a way to reflect the divine aspect within themselves — Muir stressed the systematic character of the natural world and the resulting importance of protecting such vital resources as forests and water supply. He also stressed the crucial role of wilderness for recreation and uplifting the human spirit: "Everybody needs beauty as well as bread, places to play in and pray in, where nature may heal and give strength to body and soul alike."[4]

In books such as *Our National Parks* (1901) and *The Yosemite* (1912), Muir traced the impact on America's wildlands of activities like sheep and cattle grazing. In this way, he influenced his contemporaries, including President Theodore Roosevelt, to establish a series of conservation programs and to create Yosemite National Park. Muir also was involved in establishing the Sequoia, Mount Rainier, Petrified Forest and Grand Canyon national parks. In 1892, he and his colleagues founded the Sierra Club, which has had a lasting influence on conservation issues, to "do something for wildness and make the mountains glad."[5]

Following Muir's lead, the 1940s American conservationist Aldo Leopold extended the notion of nature as not merely a mirror and teacher but an ecosystem directly tied to our survival. For Leopold, conservation called for an ethical approach based on respect for the environment.

In his essay, "The Land Ethic," in *A Sand County Almanac* (1949) he stated:

> An ethic may be regarded as a mode of guidance for meeting ecological situations so new or intricate, or involving such deferred reactions, that the path of social expediency is not discernible to the average individual. Animal instincts are modes of guidance for the individual in meeting such situations. Ethics are possibly a kind of community instinct in-the-making.[6]

Although this was written over fifty years ago, Leopold's vision still stands as a milestone whose sensibility and concern for ethics underlie and inform the Sustainability Revolution today.[7]

American writer and naturalist Rachel Carson's publication of *Silent Spring* in 1962 set off an alarm heard through all levels of society. Carson's depiction of the devastating impact of toxins and pollutants on the environment caused the general public and government agencies to reevaluate the limits of ecosystems. Her description of the dangers of agricultural pesticides for animals and humans made clear that our survival is linked to the viability of ecosystems.

Seminal works such as *A Sand County Almanac* and *Silent Spring* became icons in the environmental field and were adopted by the Sustainability Revolution because of their powerful fusion of environment and ethics. The ecological awareness raised by Carson and other environmentalists in the 1960s culminated in 1970 with the first Earth Day, which attracted over 20 million people to enthusiastic and peaceful rallies throughout the United States.[8]

Senator Gaylord Nelson of Wisconsin, founder of the first Earth Day, called for a national "Environmental Teach-in" aimed mostly at college campuses. The event became what he later called a "grassroots explosion." In Nelson's view, the success of Earth Day stemmed from "the spontaneous, enthusiastic response at the grassroots. Nothing like it had ever happened before .... They simply organized themselves. That was the remarkable thing that became Earth Day."[9]

Earth Day served to educate the general public about the impact of industrial society on the environment. It also began the process that led the US government to pass laws such as the Clean Air Act and the Clean Water Act protecting the environment and to establish regulatory agencies including the Environmental Protection Agency (EPA), whose purpose was to monitor more closely the environmental impact of business and industry.

Thus, "pre-sustainability" environmentalism created significant constituencies at both the popular and the official levels and united four dominant concerns: 1) an awareness of the profound spiritual links between human beings and the natural world; 2) a deep understanding of the biological interconnection of all parts of nature, including human beings; 3) an abiding concern with the potential damage of human impact on the environment; and 4) a strongly held commitment to make ethics an integral part of all environmental activism.

Contemporary Environmentalism: The Roots of Sustainability

A landmark event in the history of contemporary environmentalism was the 1972 United Nations Conference on the Human Environment in Stockholm, Sweden. This gathering internationalized the concerns of the American Earth Day events and focused on the regional pollution, especially the acid rain problems, of northern Europe.

Even more important, the Stockholm conference marked the first step toward what we see today as the Sustainability Revolution. This global forum began the attempt to find positive links between environmental concerns and economic issues such as development, growth and employment.[10] As a result of the Stockholm conference, numerous national environmental protection agencies were established, as well as the United Nations Environment Programme (UNEP), whose mission is to "provide leadership and encourage partnerships in caring for the environment by inspiring, informing and enabling nations and people to improve their quality of life without compromising that of future generations."[11]

During the 1970s Wes Jackson of The Land Institute and other pioneers brought to light the significance of sustainable practices. By the late 1970s the disposal of hazardous materials by burning them or dumping them underground or into waterways had become unacceptable. The "out of sight, out of mind" approach to toxic waste disposal, culminating in the contamination of Love Canal, where President Jimmy Carter declared a State of Emergency in 1978, spawned the creation by the US Congress of the Comprehensive Environmental Response, Compensation and Liability Act of 1980 (CERCLA), commonly known as Superfund. Superfund deals with identifying and cleaning up hazardous waste sites and allows residents adversely affected by these sites to sue the federal government. Superfund created a new industry in waste clean-up and restoration services.[12]

By the early 1980s, sustainability had begun to gain wider public attention, chiefly as a result of the publication of Robert Allen's *How to Save the World* (1980) and Lester Brown's *Building a Sustainable Society* (1981). Brown began with an incisive analysis of the economic predicament facing the world because of our careless inattention to, and disregard for, fundamental ecological limitations. He outlined a comprehensive strategy for moving from what he called "un-sustainable" practices to a global relationship with nature that reconfigures not only the human relationship with the Earth and its biological diversity but also the structure of values for integrating ecological and economic issues.

The Emergence of Sustainability: Brundtland (1987) and Rio (1992)

The emergence of sustainability in its contemporary form stems from the UN's creation in 1983 of The World Commission on Environment and Development (WCED), headed by Gro Harlem Brundtland, former prime minister of Norway.

The General Assembly asked the commission:

- to propose long-term environmental strategies for achieving sustainable development by the year 2000 and beyond;
- to recommend ways concern for the environment may be translated into greater cooperation among developing countries and between countries at different stages of economic and social development and lead to the achievement of common and mutually supportive objectives that take account of the interrelationships between people, resources, environment, and development;
- to consider ways and means by which the international community can deal more effectively with environmental concerns; and
- to help define shared perceptions of long-term environmental issues and the appropriate efforts needed to deal successfully with

the problems of protecting and enhancing the environment, a long-term agenda for action during the coming decades, and aspirational goals for the world community.[13]

In 1984 Worldwatch Institute published its first *State of the World* annual report. This report provided a global perspective on the relation between the world's resource base and the dynamics of economic development: "We are living beyond our means, largely by borrowing against the future."[14] Subsequent Worldwatch annual reports helped create a global consciousness about the interconnection of ecological, economic and social issues — an awareness soon thrust into international prominence by the publication of the Brundtland report, *Our Common Future*, in 1987.

▼

The most remembered quote from the Brundtland report defined sustainable development as "development that meets the needs of the present without compromising the ability of future generations to meet their own needs."

▲

The most remembered quote from the Brundtland report defined sustainable development as "development that meets the needs of the present without compromising the ability of future generations to meet their own needs."[15] While this definition undoubtedly is important, the Brundtland report helped define the Sustainability Revolution in two even more significant ways. Institutionally, it created the first framework for concerted action to protect the Earth's life support systems while promoting both economic and social justice goals. Conceptually, the report contained the first articulation of the key to contemporary sustainability — the importance of evaluating any proposed initiative with reference to the interaction of three fundamental criteria: ecology/environment, economy/employment and equity/equality, known today as the Three Es.

> Ecology and economy are becoming ever more interwoven — locally, regionally, nationally, and globally

into a seamless net of causes and effects.[16]

[S]ustainable development requires meeting the basic
needs of all and extending to all the opportunity to
fulfill their aspirations for a better life. A world in
which poverty is endemic will always be prone to
ecological and other [i.e., economic] catastrophes.[17]

Hence, our inability to promote the common interest in sustainable development is often a product of
the relative neglect of economic and social justice
within and amongst nations.[18]

In 1992, five years after the publication of the Brundtland
report, the United Nations Conference on Environment and
Development (UNCED), known as the Earth Summit, took place
in Rio de Janeiro, Brazil. The Earth Summit brought together more
than 180 world leaders — delegates from UN agencies and international organizations — as well as world media and hundreds of
nongovernmental organizations to build on the 1972 Stockholm
conference and the 1987 Brundtland report.

Those attending the Earth Summit agreed to the 27 principles
on environment and development of the Rio Declaration — which
"made it plain that we can no longer think of environment and economic and social development as isolated fields" — and adopted a
global program for action on sustainable development through
Agenda 21:

A comprehensive blueprint for a global partnership,
Agenda 21 strives to reconcile the twin requirements
of a high quality environment and a healthy economy for all people of the world, while identifying key
areas of responsibility as well as offering preliminary
cost estimates for success.[19]

The Earth Summit also generated: 1) the Statement of Principles
on the Management, Conservation and Sustainable Development of

All Types of Forests; 2) the UN Framework Convention on Climate Change; 3) the UN Convention on Biological Diversity; and 4) a recommendation for an international convention on desertification.[20]

Following the Earth Summit, President Bill Clinton in 1993 established the President's Council on Sustainable Development (PCSD), headed by Ray Anderson, chairman and CEO of Interface, Inc. Building on the work of the Earth Summit, the Council provided a domestic agenda for sustainable development. The mission of the PCSD was to:

- Forge consensus on policy by bringing together diverse interests to identify and develop innovative economic, environmental and social policies and strategies;
- Demonstrate implementation of policy that fosters sustainable development by working with diverse interests to identify and demonstrate implementation of sustainable development;
- Get the word out about sustainable development; and
- Evaluate and report on progress by recommending national, community, and enterprise level frameworks for tracking sustainable development.[21]

In 1999, after more than 40 public meetings and workshops, the Council completed its third and final report, *Towards a Sustainable America: Advancing Prosperity, Opportunity, and a Healthy Environment for the 21st Century*. The report recommended 140 actions that aimed to "improve our economy, protect our environment, and improve our quality of life. Many of these actions address important current issues like sprawl, climate change, urban renewal, and corporate environmental responsibility."[22]

In 2002 the World Summit on Sustainable Development (WSSD) conference was held in Johannesburg, South Africa, with the intention of having a review ten years after the 1992 Earth Summit in Rio. The outcomes of the conference included a Plan of Implementation and The Johannesburg Declaration on Sustainable Development. The Plan of Implementation designed a means for acting on the topics discussed at the Earth Summit, such as poverty eradication, consumption and production issues and health concerns. The Johannesburg Declaration emphasized the current issues facing the world community and the significance of multilateralism and practical implementation strategies.[23]

> ▼
>
> **At the global level,**
>
> **sustainability is oriented**
>
> **toward solutions that do not**
>
> **doom developing countries**
>
> **to a permanently secondary**
>
> **place in the world economy**
>
> **under the rubric of**
>
> **"environmental protection."**
>
> ▲

Whereas the Rio summit focused on the environmental issues of sustainability, the WSSD conference more effectively integrated economic and equity issues into the discussions. WSSD also included greater participation from women, youth, nongovernmental organizations and scientists.[24] The establishment of partnerships known as Type II Partnerships was supported at WSSD as another vehicle for effective program implementation.

In reviewing these key conferences and milestones, we see how the Sustainability Revolution became a diverse, worldwide, multicultural and multiperspective revolution built around the Three Es: 1) ecology/environment; 2) economy/employment; and 3) equity/equality. We now are in a position to examine these Three Es and their structural interaction while also introducing what might be considered the Fourth E: education.

The Core of Contemporary Sustainability: The Three Es

We will be using the term "sustainability" in two senses. On the one hand, it will refer to the multifaceted revolution based on the Three Es and their simultaneous interaction. On the other hand, the term will refer to the ever-evolving body of ideas, observations and hypotheses about the myriad challenges to which the revolution is seen as a creative response.

In this dual context, the key innovation of sustainability is its expansion of the earlier focus of environmentalism on the preservation and management of ecology/environment (the First E) to include on an equal basis issues related to economy/employment (the Second E) and equity/equality (the Third E). Because of this expanded focus, the Sustainability Revolution offers the possibility of a much broader coalition for positive change both within and among societies. Rather than pitting "tree huggers" against lumberjacks — so often the trope of environmental discourse — sustainability seeks a context in which the legitimate interests of all parties can be satisfied to a greater or lesser extent, always within the framework of concern for equity.

At the global level, sustainability is oriented toward solutions that do not doom developing countries to a permanently secondary place in the world economy under the rubric of "environmental protection." If, for example, the industrial nations want Brazil to stop the catastrophic decimation of the Amazon rainforest, they must help Brazil find an alternative path to economic development — preferably one that will contribute to the eradication of the brutal *favelas* in which so many poor Brazilians live.

With this background understood, we now can turn to a brief examination of each of the Three Es.

The first E: ecology/environment

There are three crucial issues in ecological sustainability: 1) short-term versus long-term perspective; 2) piecemeal versus systemic understanding of the indispensability of ecosystems for the viability of human existence; and 3) the concept of built-in limits to the human impact that ecosystems can sustain.

Environmental sustainability requires the long-term viability of our resource use, especially in areas such as resource extraction, agriculture, transportation, manufacturing and building. At the same time, civilized human existence necessarily includes such basics as clean air and water, heating and cooling and food that is safe to eat — all of which are dependent on the successful functioning of major ecosystems.

In this context, the concept of ecosystem services becomes significant. Broadly speaking, these can be defined as "the conditions and processes through which natural ecosystems, and the species that make them up, sustain and fulfill human life .... These services include purification of air and water; mitigation of floods and droughts; detoxification and decomposition of wastes ... [and] pollination of crops and natural vegetation ...."[25]

The existence of limits on ecosystems can be simply illustrated by the ecological crisis and long-term economic dislocation created by the destruction of oceans by overfishing, forests by clearcutting and fresh water by toxins and pollutants.

The second E: economy/employment

Economic sustainability departs from traditional environmentalism in its recognition of the importance of providing secure, long-term employment without jeopardizing the health of ecosystems. Creating a healthy environment, free of pollution and toxic waste, and simultaneously providing the basis for a dynamic economy that will endure for an extended period are viewed as complementary rather than conflicting endeavors.

It is crucial to note that what Paul Hawken and Amory and Hunter Lovins call "natural capital, made up of resources, living systems and ecosystem services" is as important for economic development as the more conventionally recognized human, financial and manufactured forms of capital.[26] By pointing out this key (though often ignored) aspect of economic development, sustainability makes a more realistic assessment of the dynamics of long-term economic activity than does conventional economics — an achievement made all the more powerful and appealing by a simultaneous awareness of the need for social justice.

The third E: equity/equality[27]

This third aspect of sustainability adds a sense of community to the existing mix of ecologically based, long-term economic development. Community-building recognizes the importance of coopera-tion and concern for one's neighbor. At a fundamental level, members of a sustainable community understand that the well-being of the individual and the larger community are interdependent. Social cohesion, compassion and tolerance are more likely to thrive in an environment where all members of the community feel that their contribution to the whole is appreciated and where an equi-table distribution of resources is recognized as essential for the long-term viability of the society.

At the level of the nation-state, equity/equality addresses the fair distribution of such resources as food, affordable housing, health care, education, job training and professional opportunities. Globally, inequities such as famine and homelessness are seen as problems of distribution rather than lack of resources. Just and equitable resource allocation is not simply ethical but essential for the well-being of the larger community — in this case, the entire world.

The three Es plus one: education[28]

The Three Es and their interaction are made even more powerful by an active commitment to public education. Education is the catalyst for helping everyone understand the dynamic nature of the interre-lationship of the Three Es. Through education we gain knowledge with which to overcome the cognitive and normative — and hence emotional — obstacles to understanding our global dilemma. Through education, sustainability can become firmly established within the existing value structure of societies while simultaneously helping that value structure evolve toward a more viable long-term approach to systemic global problems.

The Methodology: Fundamental Principles

It is in this context of the Three Es Plus One that we turn to the question of how to create a nuanced, dynamic and multidimension-al portrait of the Sustainability Revolution today.

This endeavor can best be undertaken through an analysis of the fundamental principles that each organization identifying itself with sustainability lays out at the beginning of its public self-definition — whether in brochures, booklets and other standard media or on websites in cyberspace.

Why focus on fundamental principles? By definition, a principle is "a guiding sense of the requirements and obligations of right conduct."[29] A statement of principles provides the "guiding sense," or basic direction, that any organization will use in orienting itself to the world and in making decisions in concrete situations. Principles play a key role in setting the context for the ethical choices that organizations make.

The focus on principles can help us make sense of sustainability in the wake of the explosion of groups identifying themselves with the revolution since the publication of the Brundtland report in 1987. The flowering of organizations worldwide claiming adherence to sustainability illustrates the popularity of this self-identification. An Internet search on any aspect of sustainability yields thousands of individuals, organizations and government agencies professing allegiance to sustainable practices. The best way to gain a well-rounded perspective on their multiple viewpoints is to focus on the fundamental principles these groups articulate.

We see five reasons to focus on these fundamental principles:

1. A statement of principles is almost always one of the first messages these groups present and therefore would seem very important to the groups themselves.

2. Although in some cases there are gaps, there is a critical structural connection between the principles and the actions these groups attempt to take.

3. These principles present the authors' perspectives in their own words.

4. Examining statements of principles is a convenient and concise tool for the analysis of sustainability as a whole.

5. To the best of our knowledge, this is the first comprehensive analytical study of these statements of principles.

Criteria for Selecting Principles[30]

We have used five criteria for selecting the organizations and individuals whose fundamental principles we will examine. These criteria are:

1. obtaining a wide range of viewpoints on sustainability

2. including perspectives from individuals, organizations and government agencies

3. incorporating cross-cultural viewpoints on sustainability by examining work done by groups from a variety of different cultures and nation-states

4. examining industries that have a close association with our basic human needs (such as food, shelter and energy) and natural resources (such as petroleum, wood and fisheries)

5. including sustainability perspectives from various levels — local, regional, national, global and from diverse fields of endeavor including science, philosophy, business and architecture

Using these criteria, we have chosen to analyze sustainability principles in five basic categories. These are:

1. community

2. commerce

3. natural resources

4. ecological design

5. the biosphere

Although education originally was designated as a distinct category, it has been integrated into all the others. Since it provides a way to understand and evaluate the perspectives of all the principles, education is at the foundation of sustainability.[31]

Principles as Songlines

For millennia, the Australian Aborigines have relied on a system of Songlines, tracks created by their ancestors that define the physical landscape and serve as guideposts during their travels. These landmarks conjure stories illustrating the laws the Aborigines try to follow for living with nature and navigating their seemingly barren and inhospitable land.

They refer to the Songlines as the "Way of the Law" or the "Footprints of the Ancestors" — providing both a land ethic and a compass for connecting in a harmonious way with the land and their communities, current and past:

> [E]ach totemic ancestor, while travelling through the country, was thought to have scattered a trail of words and musical notes along the line of his footprints, and ... these Dreaming-tracks lay over the land as 'ways' of communication between the most far flung tribes .... A song ... was both map and direction-finder. Providing you knew the song you could always find your way across country .... In theory, at least, the whole of Australia could be read as a musical score. There was hardly a rock or creek in the country that could not [be] or had not been sung. One should perhaps visualize the Songlines as a spaghetti of Iliads and Odysseys, writhing this way and that, in which every 'episode' was readable in terms of geology.[32]

The principles of sustainability are like the Songlines of the Aborigines. They represent the footprints of the various groups that make up the Sustainability Revolution. Like the Songlines, these statements of principles articulate a group's values, archive its history and indicate the future direction of its actions. Understanding these statements can shed light on the motivations of the groups in the Sustainability Revolution and provide a way of tracking the evolution of their core values over time. Like the Songlines, then, statements of principles act as both a tracking device — describing the route already traveled — and a compass — pointing the way to the future.

CHAPTER 2

Sustainability and Community

A community is like a ship; everyone ought to be prepared to take the helm.
                                                                    —Henrik Ibsen

Do not wait for leaders; do it alone, person to person.
                                                                    —Mother Teresa

Interdependence at All Levels

THE INTEGRATION OF SUSTAINABILITY AND COMMUNITY requires a systems perspective focused on the relationships among numerous stakeholders. At the local level, sustainable strategies involve issues such as transportation, jobs, housing, healthcare, education and the arts. At the regional level, sustainable strategies may deal with the impact of surrounding communities and available resources on an area's economic development. At the national and international levels, government policies on energy, food, healthcare and taxes may play a significant role in promoting or hindering sustainable strategies. There is an interdependence at all community levels.

The Sustainability and Community principles encompass all of the Three Es (ecology, economy and equity) because they grapple with difficult problems whose long-term solutions require a systemic approach. By addressing sustainability issues at all levels, these principles are tailored for local, regional, national and international communities.

The principles we will explore include: the Ontario Round Table on Environment and Economy (ORTEE) Model Principles (local); the Minnesota Planning Environmental Quality Board's Principles of Sustainable Development for Minnesota (regional); The Netherlands National Environmental Policy Plan (NEPP) (national); and the Earth Charter Commission's Earth Charter (international).

▼

The Sustainability and Community principles come from documents created by working groups and task forces whose aim was to create a strategy for implementing sustainable solutions to pressing environmental, economic and social problems.

▲

The ORTEE principles represent a conceptual blueprint for local communities to follow to develop strategies for sustainability. ORTEE, though vague on specific implementation methods, outlines some of the common topics, including growth, environmental limits and energy demands, that local communities inevitably confront in striving for sustainable development.

At the regional level, the Minnesota principles stand at the forefront of innovative regional green plans. Under the leadership of former Governor Arne H. Carlson, Minnesotans successfully articulated a vision for sustainable development and established implementation and tracking methods, such as the Progress Indicators, to attain their vision.[1]

At the national level, the NEPP illustrates one of the most successful examples to date of a nation's commitment to embracing and successfully implementing sustainable development policies. In some respects, the Dutch goal of achieving sustainability (though still in progress) is reminiscent of the American commitment to landing on the moon in the 1960s. The NEPP's partnership of the public and private sectors is a model of cooperation based on an integrated approach that considers the intricate relationship of the Three Es.

Finally, the Earth Charter illustrates the international community's attempt to draft a document outlining sustainability themes that will achieve consensus among all United Nations members. The result is a well-intentioned utopian, yet conceptually diffuse, vision of international harmony relying on international agreements for its implementation. The Charter's broad-stroke look at the sustainability issues from an international perspective may be a necessary first step before nations can agree on common goals, yet it would benefit greatly from the practical approach of the NEPP and Minnesota principles.

The Sustainability and Community principles come from documents created by working groups and task forces whose aim was to create a strategy for implementing sustainable solutions to pressing environmental, economic and social problems. These principles act as guideposts for specific actions undertaken by the various stakeholders. The principles also demonstrate effective partnerships of government, industries, schools and private citizens.

Ontario Round Table on Environment and Economy (ORTEE) Model Principles

The themes explored by the Ontario Round Table on Environment and Economy Model Principles attempt to provide a framework for local communities to use in defining their sustainable development goals. Regional institutions play an important role in assisting local communities to implement sustainability programs is areas such as energy, transportation and waste disposal.

The ORTEE principles are a Canadian framework intended to serve as a touchstone for any community interested in developing sustainability initiatives.

ORTEE model principles[2]

A sustainable community is one which:

1. Recognizes that growth occurs within some limits and is ultimately limited by the carrying capacity of the environment;

2. Values cultural diversity;

3. Has respect for other life forms and supports biodiversity;

4. Has shared values amongst the members of the community (promoted through sustainability education);

5. Employs ecological decision-making (e.g., integration of environmental criteria into all municipal/ government, business and personal decision-making processes);

6. Makes decisions and plans in a balanced, open and flexible manner that includes the perspectives from the social, health, economic and environmental sectors of the community;

7. Makes best use of local efforts and resources (nurtures solutions at the local level);

8. Uses renewable and reliable sources of energy;

9. Minimizes harm to the natural environment;

10. Fosters activities which use materials in continuous cycles.

And as a result, a sustainable community:

11. Does not compromise the sustainability of other communities (a geographic perspective);

12. Does not compromise the sustainability of future generations by its activities (a temporal perspective).

By focusing on limits to growth, carrying capacity, biodiversity and ecological decision making, the ORTEE principles articulate the significance of ecological factors, which all communities must address in their planning process. The ORTEE principles also point to the importance of seeking solutions at the local level to benefit from local knowledge and to work directly with stakeholders for their empowerment.

These principles acknowledge the potential impact of local decisions on neighboring communities and emphasize the interdependence of these communities. In examining the potential detrimental effects of one community on another, we also must investigate the potential benefits of working with one's neighbors. Sharing resources such as energy and water demands close cooperation, which can be an effective strategy for everyone concerned.

The ORTEE principles look at the impact of local decisions on future generations. This "temporal perspective" underscores a frequent theme in sustainability principles. The creation of shared values in the local community, promoted through sustainability education, also speaks to a long-term process of fostering consensus.

The ORTEE principles provide a flexible framework for outlining sustainability values at a wide range — from a small town to a large metropolitan city. One of the success stories of the ORTEE framework was its use for the City of Ottawa's Official Plan.

Principles of Sustainable Development for Minnesota

While the ORTEE principles create a basis for local communities to achieve consensus on sustainability values, the Principles of Sustainable Development for Minnesota attempt to find common ground on these values at a regional level.

The Minnesota principles tackle the complex sustainability issues with a comprehensive vision that includes the ecological, economic and equity concerns. The Minnesota principles were developed in 1998 by the Minnesota Round Table on Sustainable Development, a group of 30 community leaders appointed by former Governor Arne H. Carlson to:

> consider how Minnesotans can safeguard their long-
> term environmental, economic and social well-being

> ... to serve as a catalyst for sustainable development,
> to foster public and private partnerships and reach
> out to Minnesotans across the state, and to stimulate
> interest in and communicate the importance of
> achieving sustainable development."[3]

As a guide for achieving these objectives, the following principles were devised.

Principles of sustainable development for Minnesota[4]

The Minnesota Round Table on Sustainable Development offers five principles as guideposts along the path of sustainable development. They are:

1. **Global interdependence.** Economic prosperity, ecosystem health, liberty and justice are linked, and our long-term well-being depends on maintaining all four. Local decisions must be informed by their regional and global context.

2. **Stewardship.** Stewardship requires the recognition that we are all caretakers of the environment and economy for the benefit of present and future generations. We must balance the impacts of today's decisions with the needs of future generations.

3. **Conservation.** Minnesotans must maintain essential ecological processes, biological diversity and life-support systems of the environment; harvest renewable resources on a sustainable basis; and make wise and efficient use of our renewable and non-renewable resources.

4. **Indicators.** Minnesotans need to have and use clear goals and measurable indicators based on reliable information to guide public policies and private actions toward long-term economic prosperity, community vitality, cultural diversity and healthy ecosystems.

5. **Shared responsibility.** All Minnesotans accept responsibility for sustaining the environment and economy, with each being accountable for his or her decisions and actions, in a spirit of partnership and open cooperation. No entity has the right to shift the costs of its behavior to other individuals, communities, states, nations or future generations. Full-cost accounting is essential for assuring shared responsibility.

The goal of the Minnesota principles is to maintain a strong economy while simultaneously preserving the environment. As the report states: "The Round Table's recommendations are based on the recognition that Minnesotans do not need or want to choose between good jobs, vital communities and a healthy environment. They want all three."[5] These principles represent one of the first statewide initiatives for achieving a sustainable development plan in the United States.[6] As a leader in this area, Minnesota has developed a blueprint for bringing together the various stakeholders to discuss the relevant issues and work toward consensus.

One of the key concepts in the Minnesota principles is that of "global interdependence." Global interdependence highlights the importance of looking at the regional and global context when making local decisions. Local traffic patterns, for example, often are connected to the regional infrastructure, which in turn may be dependent on employees working for transnational corporations with global interests.

The Minnesota principles also incorporate tools for measuring progress. Measurable indicators are described as a tool to "guide public policies and private actions toward long-term economic prosperity, community vitality, cultural diversity and healthy ecosystems." The reference to indicators speaks to the implementation strategy for the sustainability plan.

While including the concept of indicators will help residents understand how to tell if goals are being achieved, indicators are an assessment tool that should not be confused with principles. In fact, indicators rely on principles for criteria in obtaining relevant data.

inciples of Sustainable Development for Minnesota refer to
1 ne Bellagio Principles for Assessment, which serve as a guide for
choosing and interpreting indicators.[7]

Sustainability indicators have been widely used by local communities as a measurement tool. In Seattle, Washington, for example,
the sustainability indicators program first developed by Sustainable
Seattle in the early 1990s has since become an important method for
other cities and neighborhoods to use to measure their environmental, economic and social health.[8] One of the challenges of
implementing indicators lies in managing environmental or social
factors that may extend beyond a local community's control.
Indicators ranging from air and water quality to affordable housing,
unemployment, juvenile crime and arts programs have been used by
local communities worldwide as a means for members from all sectors of society to come together to define and monitor the trends
affecting their quality of life.

The "shared responsibility" section of the Minnesota principles
provides a refreshing outlook on the importance of personal responsibility, cooperation and partnership in sustainable development
solutions. This section squarely challenges the NIMBY (Not In My
Back Yard) attitude often encountered in regional issues. The costs
of solving environmental, economic and social problems are to be
passed on neither to other entities nor to future generations. "Full-
cost accounting" encourages a collaborative spirit of sharing
responsibility and resources.

The Minnesota principles focus on the conservation of biodiversity, the use of renewable resources, and a long-term view to provide
a healthy ecosystem for future generations. As a pioneering statewide
plan, the Principles of Sustainable Development for Minnesota represent an important contribution to the promotion of sustainable
values beyond the local level.[9] In addition to Minnesota, the states
of New Jersey and Oregon have been in the vanguard of green plans
with New Jersey's 2001 report *Governing with the Future in Mind*
and Oregon's passage of the Sustainability Act in 2001 and its
Sustainability Plan 2004.[10]

The Netherlands National Environmental Policy Plan (NEPP)

At a national level, environmental policy plans, or green plans, provide a concerted approach for linking local and regional sustainability issues to a national agenda. The Dutch environmental policy plan is a series of evolving strategies for integrating the Three Es of sustainability:

> This "green plan" is much more than a series of regulations — it is a comprehensive strategy for sustainable development that explores the economic and social concerns of maintaining a healthy environment. The NEPP looks not only at specific pollution sources, but their relationship to relevant ecological, social, and economic systems.[11]

The NEPP is part of a growing number of national green plans currently under development, including New Zealand's Resource Management Act, Canada's Green Plan and the Mexican Environmental Program. All of these plans look at national strategies for achieving sustainable development.

The NEPP was enacted in 1989 and has been updated every four years. NEPP4, published in June 2001, focuses "mainly on areas where people perceive a real relationship between quality of life and the environment, and where in addition Dutch actions can impact the quality of life in other countries. Quality of life will be the guiding principle in making policy."[12] In contrast to previous Dutch plans, NEPP4 addresses the impacts of a globalized world economy in which environmental problems such as climate change, loss of biodiversity and pollution have become increasingly internationalized. In addition, NEPP4 looks ahead to the year 2030, recognizing the importance of a longer-term perspective in devising an effective policy direction.[13] A summary of the principles from the NEPP outlines a comprehensive approach to the key concerns of an industrial society.

The major principles from the NEPP[14]

- **Intergenerational equity:** The current generation is responsible for providing a sustainable environment for the next generation.

- **The precautionary principle:** In light of uncertainties, it is best not to make decisions that may involve serious environmental risks.

- **The standstill principle:** As an absolute minimum, environmental conditions shall not further deteriorate.

- **Abatement at source:** Harmful environmental actions should be prevented at their source.

- **The polluter pays principle:** Internalization of environmental costs through such means as licensing fees, environmental taxes.

- **Use of the best applicable technology** to control pollution and other environmental harms.

- **Prevention** of all unnecessary waste.

- **Isolation, management, and control** of wastes that cannot be processed.

- **Internalization:** Environmental considerations are to be integrated into the actions of all responsible groups.

- **Integrated lifecycle management:** Manufacturers are responsible for all environmental impacts of their products, from manufacture to use to disposal. Waste flows and pollution should be reduced at all stages.

- **Environmental space:** Recognizes a limit to the level of resources each person can consume if society is to be environmentally sustainable. This concept was first introduced by the environmental group Milieudefensie (the Dutch version of Friends of the Earth) and was incorporated into the second NEPP.

Many of the principles in the NEPP examine the potential damage caused by unwise or ignorant decisions by the industrial sector. The "precautionary principle," for example, calls for no action if there is any doubt as to the potential consequences.[15] Past environmental disasters such as the use of DDT might have been avoided by following this principle. Adhering to the precautionary principle might also have prevented the current nuclear waste disposal problem we face around the world.

The "standstill principle" — whereby we commit ourselves to doing nothing that will further deteriorate the environment — also recognizes the potentially devastating effects of our actions. The standstill principle encourages intervention only if it will improve a situation, such as an environmental restoration project.

The "abatement at source" principle calls for elimination of damaging effects — from industrial production, for example — at their source. Source reduction deals with waste by not creating it in the first place.

"Integrated lifecycle management" aims to reduce waste by making manufacturers responsible for the full life of their products. Thus, automobile makers would be required to take back and recycle their vehicles. Some European automobile manufacturers, such as BMW, already have implemented aspects of the integrated lifecycle management principle.

The NEPP principles also focus on ways of reducing the impact of pollution. The "polluter pays" and the "use of the best applicable technology to control pollution and other environmental harms" principles highlight a firm commitment by the Dutch government to control pollution. Environmental taxes, for example, provide an appropriate method for controlling pollution by targeting companies that are directly involved in environmentally damaging activities. Encouraging the invention and use of technology for pollution prevention creates a climate for innovative and cost-effective solutions to flourish.

The NEPP addresses the social aspects of sustainability through the "intergenerational equity" and "environmental space" principles.

Intergenerational equity emphasizes the common theme of our responsibility for providing a sustainable environment for future generations. Environmental space addresses posting "a limit to the level of resources each person can consume if society is to be environmentally sustainable." This principle brings the issues of sustainability to the personal level and shows us each how our consumption decisions impact sustainability. The issue of personal consumption raises numerous questions. Who is to decide what the limit of personal consumption should be? And what criteria should be used to set the limit?

An innovative tool devised to gauge our consumption of nature's resources is the Ecological Footprint.[16] Devised in 1990 by Mathis Wackernagel and William Rees, the Ecological Footprint "tracks how much individuals, organizations, cities, regions, nations or humanity as a whole consume and compares this amount to the resources nature can provide."[17] The City of London; the National Assembly of Wales; the State of Victoria, Australia; and Sonoma County, California, all have used the Ecological Footprint to determine human impact on the environment. As a result of its Ecological Footprint report, Sonoma became the first US county to commit to reducing its CO_2 emissions by 20 percent.[18]

The NEPP principles reflect the fact that The Netherlands is a highly industrialized society. The principles dealing with pollution and waste management underscore the issues facing the Dutch. The Netherlands has the second highest population density in the world (after Bangladesh) and about one third of its land is reclaimed from the sea and lies below sea level.[19] The Dutch public are very much aware of environmental limits, and in partnership with government agencies have developed a green plan that is making a difference in finding lasting sustainable solutions.

As part of a comprehensive green plan, the NEPP principles have set an international standard because of the effective cooperation and consensus between the public and private sectors and the involvement of citizens in making changes for sustainability. The NEPP shows how principles can guide a nation's environmental policy. As stated in NEEP4's summary, "Above all, with this policy document we want to make clear that sustainable living is possible while avoiding socially unacceptable results. One thing is clear: it pays to have good policies."[20]

The Earth Charter

The Earth Charter principles provide a comprehensive, multidimensional approach to presenting values for worldwide acceptance. Although the principles cover a wide range of sustainability issues, they fall short on practical implementation strategies. However, the importance of the Earth Charter lies in its attempt to achieve global consensus.

Completed in 2000, the Earth Charter represents the culmination of a decade's work by individuals and organizations some of whose objectives were:

- to promote a worldwide dialogue on shared values and global ethics;

- to circulate the Earth Charter throughout the world as a people's treaty, promoting awareness, commitment, and implementation of Earth Charter values;

- to seek endorsement of the Earth Charter by the United Nations General Assembly by the year 2002.[21]

The Earth Charter presents sustainability ideals in the form of a declaration. The "Preamble" outlines the hope for the charter "to bring forth a sustainable global society founded on respect for nature, universal human rights, economic justice, and a culture of peace." The next sections cover the ecological, economic and equity aspects of sustainability. Finally, "The Way Forward" seeks to clarify a vision of sustainability for all peoples to embrace and offers hope for "a new beginning." An abbreviated version of the Earth Charter follows:[22]

The earth charter

Preamble

We stand at a critical moment in Earth's history, a time when humanity must choose its future. As the world becomes increasingly interdependent and fragile, the future at once holds great peril and great promise. To move forward we must recognize that in the midst of a magnificent diversity of cultures and life forms we are one human family and one Earth community with a common destiny. We must join together to bring forth a sustainable global society founded on respect for nature, universal human rights, economic justice, and a culture of peace. Towards this end, it is imperative that we, the peoples of Earth, declare our responsibility to one another, to the greater community of life, and to future generations.

Earth, Our Home

Humanity is part of a vast evolving universe. Earth, our home, is alive with a unique community of life. The forces of nature make existence a demanding and uncertain adventure, but Earth has provided the conditions essential to life's evolution.

The Global Situation

The dominant patterns of production and consumption are causing environmental devastation, the depletion of resources, and a massive extinction of species. Communities are being undermined.

The Challenges Ahead

The choice is ours: form a global partnership to care for Earth and one another or risk the destruction of ourselves and the diversity of life. Fundamental changes are needed in our values, institutions, and ways of living.

Universal Responsibility

To realize these aspirations, we must decide to live with a sense of universal responsibility, identifying ourselves with the whole Earth community as well as our local communities.

We urgently need a shared vision of basic values to provide an ethical foundation for the emerging world community. Therefore, together in hope we affirm the following interdependent principles for a sustainable way of life as a common standard by which the conduct of all individuals, organizations, businesses, governments, and transnational institutions is to be guided and assessed.

The report next outlines 16 principles grouped into four areas of concern.

I. Respect and Care For the Community of Life

1. Respect Earth and life in all its diversity.

2. Care for the community of life with understanding, compassion, and love.

3. Build democratic societies that are just, participatory, sustainable, and peaceful.

4. Secure Earth's bounty and beauty for present and future generations.

II. Ecological Integrity

5. Protect and restore the integrity of Earth's ecological systems, with special concern for biological diversity and the natural processes that sustain life.

6. Prevent harm as the best method of environmental protection and, when knowledge is limited, apply a precautionary approach.

7. Adopt patterns of production, consumption, and reproduction that safeguard Earth's regenerative capacities, human rights, and community well-being.

8. Advance the study of ecological sustainability and promote the open exchange and wide application of the knowledge acquired.

III. Social and Economic Justice

9. Eradicate poverty as an ethical, social, and environmental imperative.

10. Ensure that economic activities and institutions at all levels promote human development in an equitable and sustainable manner.

11. Affirm gender equality and equity as prerequisites to sustainable development and ensure universal access to education, health care, and economic opportunity.

12. Uphold the right of all, without discrimination, to a natural and social environment supportive of human dignity, bodily health, and spiritual well-being, with special attention to the rights of indigenous peoples and minorities.

IV. Democracy, Nonviolence, and Peace

13. Strengthen democratic institutions at all levels, and provide transparency and accountability in governance, inclusive participation in decision making, and access to justice.

14. Integrate into formal education and life-long learning the knowledge, values, and skills needed for a sustainable way of life.

15. Treat all living beings with respect and consideration.

16. Promote a culture of tolerance, nonviolence, and peace.

The Way Forward

As never before in history, common destiny beckons us to seek a new beginning. Such renewal is the promise of these Earth Charter principles. To fulfill this promise, we must commit ourselves to adopt and promote the values and objectives of the Charter.

This requires a change of mind and heart. It requires a new sense of global interdependence and universal responsibility. We must imaginatively develop and apply the vision of a sustainable way of life locally, nationally, regionally, and globally. Our cultural diversity is a precious heritage and different cultures will find their own distinctive ways to realize the vision. We must deepen and expand the global dialogue that generated the Earth Charter, for we have much to learn from the ongoing collaborative search for truth and wisdom.

Life often involves tensions between important values. This can mean difficult choices. However, we must find ways to harmonize diversity with unity, the exercise of freedom with the common good, short-term objectives with long-term goals. Every individual, family, organization, and community has a vital role to play. The arts, sciences, religions, educational institutions, media, businesses, nongovernmental organizations, and governments are all called to offer creative leadership. The partnership of government, civil society, and business is essential for effective governance.

In order to build a sustainable global community, the nations of the world must renew their commitment to the United Nations, fulfill their obligations under existing international agreements, and support the implementation of Earth Charter principles with an international legally binding instrument on environment and development.

Let ours be a time remembered for the awakening of a new reverence for life, the firm resolve to achieve sustainability, the quickening of the struggle for justice and peace, and the joyful celebration of life.

The Earth Charter highlights basic values of sustainability such as respect for life, protection of the environment, social justice and democracy. The Charter emphasizes environmental conservation and protection for future generations. It also advocates biodiversity and the precautionary principle, already mentioned in our discussion of the NEPP principles.

Since the World Summit on Sustainable Development (WSSD) gathering in Johannesburg in 2002, the Earth Charter has developed into a significant educational tool providing a useful framework for discussing such topics as globalization, ethics and social justice. At the community level, the Earth Charter's Local Community/ Government initiative, with the collaboration of the International Council of Local Environment Initiatives (ICLEI), has encouraged municipalities to adopt the charter to promote sustainable development. To date, the charter has been endorsed by organizations such as the US Conference of Mayors (1,000 members), the Florida League of Cities (400 members) and cities including Berkeley, California; Burlington, Vermont; Urbino, Italy; San Jose, Costa Rica; and Valverde de la Vera, Spain.[23]

International Council of Local Environment Initiatives (ICLEI)

One of the more exciting international networks supporting community-based sustainable development programs is spearheaded by the International Council of Local Environment Initiatives (ICLEI). Founded in 1990 by the United Nations, ICLEI has an international membership of over 450 cities, towns, counties, metropolitan governments and local government associations. Its mission is to "build and serve a worldwide movement of local governments to achieve tangible improvements in global sustainability with special focus on environmental conditions through cumulative local actions."[24] ICLEI has generated over 6,000 initiatives in more than 100 countries ranging from home energy efficiency programs to recycling programs.[25]

Using the Earth Charter principles as a guiding framework, ICLEI's members work on campaigns including Local Agenda 21 (LA21), the Water Campaign and Cities for Climate Protection (CCP). Each of these campaigns involves close cooperation to develop performance milestones, strategies and partnerships to achieve objectives. The LA21 campaign, which grew out of the

World Summit on Sustainable Development in 2002, has over 2,000 communities worldwide dedicated to achieving a planning process that promotes tangible results for local sustainable development initiatives. The Water Campaign's goal is to improve the use of fresh water resources and alleviate the global water crisis through protection of watersheds, pollution reduction and improving water treatment methods.

The Cities for Climate Protection campaign aims to reduce global warming and air pollution emissions. There are over 500 local governments, representing 8 percent of global gas emissions, participating in the program.[26] Through technical assistance, training and marketing tools, the CCP campaign is an important first step in establishing an international network for reducing carbon dioxide and methane levels. In the United States over 140 cities and counties currently participate in the CCP campaign, and in 2002 Sonoma County, California, became the first county to have 100 percent of its local governments join the program.

Integrating Sustainability Values at All Community Levels

The Sustainability and Community principles serve as important policy guidelines for stakeholders to use as a foundation in identifying and implementing their vision of sustainable development. Following these guidelines they can incorporate a wide range of viewpoints by integrating their common interests. The principles thus provide a meaningful context for dialogue about the ecological, economic and social issues confronting communities.

The successful application of these principles rests on forging consensus on sustainability values of universal appeal that can be applied at the local, regional, national and international levels. Although the consensus approach often is plagued by prolonged discussions, it serves to educate all participants and generate a personal stake in the outcome.

CHAPTER 3

Sustainability and Commerce

The future belongs to those who understand that doing more with less is compassionate, prosperous and enduring and thus more intelligent, even competitive.

—Paul Hawken

The ability to learn faster than your competitors may be the only sustainable competitive advantage.

—Peter Senge

Beyond "Business as Usual"

THE SUSTAINABILITY REVOLUTION'S IMPACT on business represents one of the greatest changes presently taking place in society. Business activities of many multinational, medium-sized and small corporations are having a detrimental impact on natural systems, reflected in declining fish stocks, forests, water supply and agricultural yields worldwide, an increase in pollution and toxic waste and global climate change. "Business as usual" is destroying Earth's life-support systems.

The Sustainability Revolution encourages business practices to mimic natural systems. This industrial ecology perspective applies to the efficient design of products and services and the elimination of waste. Sustainable business practices are becoming recognized as essential not only for corporate survival but also for the long-term health of the planet.

In the "business as usual" approach, companies treat environmental concerns as impediments to business success. Regulatory compliance is viewed as simply another cost of doing business. Therefore, in order to avoid compromising profits the prevailing attitude is to meet only the minimum compliance requirements. The Sustainability Revolution is changing this corporate attitude by making sustainability integral to running a successful business. The service and manufacturing sectors are shifting from merely meeting environmental compliance standards to realizing the competitive advantage of devising and implementing sustainable business strategies. Instead of being seen as an impediment to business development, sustainable practices, including ecological, economic and social concerns, now are seen as business opportunities.

One of the preeminent voices in sustainable business is John Elkington, who coined the term "triple bottom line"(TBL). The triple bottom line challenges companies to look not merely at the economic or profit aspect of their business but also at the environmental and social costs:

> At its narrowest, the term 'triple bottom line' is used as a framework for measuring and reporting corporate performance against economic, social and environmental parameters. At its broadest, the term is used to capture the whole set of values, issues and processes that companies must address in order to minimize any harm resulting from their activities and to create economic, social and environmental value.[1]

Companies embracing this attitude are setting a new standard of corporate responsibility. For example, Interface, Inc., a leading commercial carpet manufacturer, goes beyond doing a traditional environmental report and publishes a corporate sustainability report — one that discusses not only environmental but also economic and social commitments to their customers and the communities where they operate.

From 1995 to 2003 Interface cumulatively saved over $231 million by eliminating waste. Interface defines waste as any cost that does not provide value to the customer. From 1996 to 2003 it reduced the total energy required to manufacture carpet by 35 percent and increased its renewable energy consumption to over 12 percent. The water intake per square meter of carpet decreased 78 percent in modular carpet facilities and 40 percent in broadloom facilities. Absolute carbon dioxide emissions were reduced by 46 percent. In Interface's quest to improve social sustainability, in 2003 its employees spent nearly 12,000 volunteer hours in community activities, and over 25 percent of its management positions were held by women employees. From 1999 to 2003, the Interface Environmental Foundation contributed nearly $110,000 to environmental education, reaching more than 20,000 students in the communities where its employees live and work.[2]

The mission at Interface, as with other leaders of sustainable business, is to devise strategies that support and restore natural systems. In its vision statement, Interface aspires "to be the first company that, by its deeds, shows the entire industrial world what sustainability is, in all its dimensions: people, process, product, place, and profits — by 2020 — and in so doing, we will become restorative through the power of influence."[3]

Adopting Sustainable Strategies

The seemingly limitless abundance of natural resources, combined with innovative manufacturing techniques and the establishment of a monetary system, provided the foundation for the birth of the industrial era. Our current commerce practices are based on an outmoded linear approach that results in resource consumption with tremendous waste and inequitable distribution of goods and services.

The unbelievable success of the business sector in exploiting the Earth's minerals, forests, oceans and species has yielded a consumption-based world economy. However, the increasing cost of scarcer resources has forced corporations to reassess their operations and seek alternative ways of conducting business. These changes, in turn, are shedding light on the economic and social costs of "business as usual."

The limits of natural resources, declining ecosystems and increasing economic disparity have given birth to sustainable practices in business. While a bounty of commodities fueled the Industrial Revolution, dwindling natural resources are calling on businesses to innovate and shift from a model based on providing manufactured goods to one that delivers value to customers and supports the well-being of local communities.

Although the Sustainability Revolution's impact on the business sector is still in its initial phase, some promising events are taking place. Prominent companies including Ford, Royal Dutch Shell, Ikea and Nike are adopting sustainability as a key strategy for charting their future development. These companies are causing a ripple effect by requiring their suppliers to adopt similar standards.

▼

The limits of natural resources, declining ecosystems and increasing economic disparity have given birth to sustainable practices in business.

▲

Companies are choosing to move forward and are promoting their sustainability strategies with guiding principles or frameworks that support their mission statement. These principles, which often evolve from conferences or publications, serve to chart a company's direction toward achieving sustainability. The principles promote environmentally friendly buildings, operations, design and manufacturing procedures as well as a socially responsible business ethic.

Several companies have devised their own sustainability assessment tools. Arup, an international engineering firm with over 7,000 employees in 32 countries, utilizes the Sustainable Project Appraisal Routine (SPeAR®) to assess sustainability performance. SPeAR focuses on indicators of environmental protection, social equity, economic viability and efficient use of natural resources to assist in managing information for making decisions on sustainability issues.

SPeAR has aided in the building design and operations of organizations ranging from the Fresno Metropolitan Museum in California to the Jaguar Halewood factory in the UK.[4]

Several trade, nonprofit, government and international organizations also have created frameworks to help companies devise and implement sustainable strategies. The Life Cycle Assessment (LCA) process provides organizations with a tool to evaluate the environmental impact of a product, process or activity by examining the energy and materials used, waste generated and ways of implementing environmental improvements.[5] In the social justice realm, the Global Sullivan Principles of Social Responsibility provide companies with a framework addressing issues of human rights and equal opportunity.[6]

Business for Social Responsibility, Social Venture Network, the International Chamber of Commerce and the Coalition for Environmentally Responsible Economies provide a means for companies to assess their environmental and social impacts. In addition, the United Nations Global Compact sets a framework for international corporate citizens, and the nongovernmental organization Global Reporting Initiative (GRI) provides guidelines voluntarily adopted by over 600 multinational corporations.[7] The GRI guidelines promote "international harmonization in the reporting of relevant and credible corporate environmental, social and economic performance information to enhance responsible decision-making."[8]

As a mechanism for reporting "material" environmental and social risks, GRI is rapidly emerging as the standard for nonfinancial reporting and provides an important avenue for legitimizing sustainability concerns in the traditional business community. Although GRI is gaining acceptance as a reporting tool, the financial markets have not yet fully embraced the importance of the environmental and social aspects of sustainable business practices. While socially responsible investors are aware of the significant value associated with a company's concern for its triple bottom line, its adoption by mainstream investors remains a challenge.[9]

In the financial sector, the Equator Principles, launched in 2003, guide financial institutions in addressing social and environmental impacts of financing development projects.[10] The Equator Principles are based on the guidelines used by the International Finance Corporation (IFC), the financial division of the World Bank. Within the first year, the Equator Principles enlisted 23 member banks from around the world, representing 80 percent of worldwide project financing.[11] Although it is perhaps too soon to evaluate the effectiveness of the Equator Principles, the dominant presence of ten of the world's largest banks, including CitiGroup, Bank of America and HSBC Holdings, is capable of having a significant impact on promoting sustainable practices for international development projects.

Using the frameworks from these and other organizations is essential for assessing the business community's progress toward sustainable practices. A company that professes "green" practices can be evaluated against widely recognized standards. These standards help people within and outside the business community to distinguish between a company making genuine progress toward sustainability and one that merely engages in green marketing slogans, or "green washing."

To better understand the values that are driving companies toward sustainability, we examine four sets of principles: the precautionary principle, the Natural Step's Four System Conditions, the Houston Principles and the Coalition for Environmentally Responsible Economies (CERES) Principles. These principles highlight the relationship of economic activities, employment and the environment. They are particularly significant because they set standards with long-lasting and far-reaching effects. The principles articulate the classic challenges of maximizing profits within the environmental limitations faced by the business community and describe an alternative approach to achieving expected returns while safeguarding the environment and social equity.

The Precautionary Principle

Though not yet widely known in the business sector, the precautionary principle challenges businesses to rethink their responsibility to society. This principle asks businesses to use foresight in the development of new products and processes and, if these are deemed potentially dangerous to society, to refrain from further action. This shift of responsibility from the consumer and government regulators to the corporation illustrates a new business ethic. This ethic recognizes a company's accountability not only to its investors but more significantly to the larger community that may be affected by its actions. The origin of the precautionary principle dates back to one of Germany's basic principles of environmental policy in the mid-1970s.[12] A German national law, known as the "precaution" or "foresight" principle, stated:

> Environmental policy is not fully accomplished by warding off imminent hazards and the elimination of damage which has occurred. Precautionary environmental policy requires furthermore that natural resources are protected and demands on them are made with care.[13]

The precautionary principle was subsequently mentioned in The Rio Declaration on the Environment (1992) and further defined when a group of scientists, government officials, lawyers and environmental representatives met at Wingspread in Racine, Wisconsin, in 1998. The Wingspread Statement augments and expands the precautionary principle as follows:

Wingspread statement on the precautionary principle[14]

The release and use of toxic substances, the exploitation of resources, and physical alterations of the environment have had substantial unintended consequences affecting human health and the environment. Some of these concerns are high rates of learning deficiencies, asthma, cancer, birth defects and species extinctions, along with global climate change, stratospheric ozone depletion and worldwide contamination with toxic substances and nuclear materials.

We believe existing environmental regulations and other decisions, particularly those based on risk assessment, have failed to protect adequately human health and the environment — the larger system of which humans are but a part.

We believe there is compelling evidence that damage to humans and the worldwide environment is of such magnitude and seriousness that new principles for conducting human activities are necessary.

While we realize that human activities may involve hazards, people must proceed more carefully than has been the case in recent history. Corporations, government entities, organizations, communities, scientists and other individuals must adopt a precautionary approach to all human endeavors.

Therefore it is necessary to implement the Precautionary Principle: Where an activity raises threats of harm to human health or the environment, precautionary measures should be taken even if some cause and effect relationships are not fully established scientifically. In this context, the proponent of an activity, rather than the public, should bear the burden of proof.

The process of applying the Precautionary Principle must be open, informed and democratic, and must include potentially affected parties. It must also involve an examination of the full range of alternatives, including no action.

The Wingspread formulation of the precautionary principle states that people have a duty to take preemptive action to prevent harm. In addition, the burden of proof of harmlessness lies with the proponents, not with the general public, and before using a new technology, process or chemical or starting a new activity "the full range of alternatives," including doing nothing, must be explored. Finally, decisions related to the precautionary principle "must include potentially affected parties" and be "open, informed and democratic."[15]

The precautionary principle challenges the process of technological innovation by calling for a thorough evaluation of the potential harm from our discoveries. In the case of cigarettes, for example, the precautionary principle would have required manufacturers to prove that cigarettes did not create a health hazard. Millions of lives might have been saved had this principle been applied when cigarettes were first manufactured instead of waiting until years after the introduction of cigarettes for the US government to prove that smoking causes cancer.

Opponents of the precautionary principle stress that it is impossible to scientifically anticipate all the potential effects of a new technology or discovery. Nevertheless, the US Food and Drug Administration (FDA) demands a much higher level of scrutiny from drug manufacturers by requiring studies that prove the safety of new drugs and treatments. Similar studies should be required in other industries.

Biotechnology is a rapidly evolving field where the precautionary principle would have a significant impact. In the development of genetically modified plants and animals, for example, the precautionary principle would place the responsibility for health and environmental safety on the manufacturers. The introduction of genetically modified salmon would be allowed to proceed only once extensive studies could prove that it poses no threat to the health of humans and other species.[16] Companies today operate at a fast pace in order to establish leadership and dominate the marketplace. The pressures of a market economy that rewards speed and dominance present a barrier to the precautionary principle.

The significance of the precautionary principle is seen through its implementation in environmental plans and international treaties such as the Rio Declaration (principle 15, 1992), the Helsinki

Convention (1992),[17] the Framework Convention on Climate Change (1992)[18] and the Cartagena Protocol on Biosafety (2000).[19]

Although the precautionary principle seems to be a logical approach for businesses that adhere to socially responsible values, many organizations still view the principle as an obstacle to techno- logical innovation. In international trade, the precautionary principle has yet to be embraced by trading institutions such as the World Trade Organization (WTO). In fact, currently a WTO mem- ber who refuses to·accept a product from a trading partner because of safety concerns must prove its hazard or face being fined for put- ting up a trade barrier. The WTO deemed illegal the European Union's ban on US beef injected with growth hormones. Although the European Union had legitimate safety concerns, it lacked defin- itive proof of a hazard.

However, the precautionary principle is being applied at the municipal level. In 2003, for example, the City of San Francisco passed the San Francisco Precautionary Principle Ordinance as a policy model for future legislation that affects the city's general wel- fare. As stated in the ordinance:

> The Board of Supervisors encourages all City employees and officials to take the precautionary principle into consideration and evaluate alternatives when taking actions that could impact health and the environment, especially where those actions could pose threats of serious harm or irreversible damage.[20]

Although it is too early to evaluate the effectiveness of this ordi- nance, whose impact will be reviewed within three years, the foresight of its implementation is exemplary.

The Natural Step

While the precautionary principle challenges the business sector to reassess its responsibility to the public, the Natural Step's scientifi- cally based "system conditions" provide a practical framework for businesses to use in applying sustainable practices. For businesses and institutions seeking to adopt well-grounded, applicable and tested sustainable practices, the Natural Step provides a useful roadmap. Already in use for over a decade, the Natural Step is an adaptable and flexible method for assessing the impact of a company's actions on a community with respect to the laws of nature.

The Natural Step was founded in 1989 by Swedish oncologist Karl-Henrik Robèrt. Robèrt's concern for the effects of the environment on his cancer patients led him to examine the environmental movement. He discovered that the debate looked mainly at the peripheral details of environmental issues rather than at the root causes of systemic problems. He used the analogy of bickering about the leaves of a tree rather than focusing on the trunk, which is the supporting structure.

After making countless revisions, Robèrt and fifty of his Swedish colleagues outlined the Natural Step's Four System Conditions for sustainability. In 1995, the Natural Step was brought to the United States by Donald W. Aitken, principal of Donald Aitken Associates, and entrepreneur and author Paul Hawken. It since has established offices in Australia, Brazil, Canada, Israel, Japan, New Zealand, South Africa, Sweden and the United Kingdom.

The natural step's four system conditions[21]

1. **In order for a society to be sustainable, nature's functions and diversity are not systematically subject to increasing concentrations of substances extracted from the earth's crust.**

   In a sustainable society, human activities such as the burning of fossil fuels and the mining of metals and minerals will not occur at a rate that causes them to systematically increase in the ecosphere. There are thresholds beyond which living organisms and ecosystems are adversely affected by increases in substances from the earth's crust. Problems may include an increase in greenhouse gases leading to global warming, contamination of surface and ground water, and metal toxicity which can cause functional disturbances in animals. In practical terms, the first condition requires society to implement comprehensive metal and mineral recycling programs, and decrease economic dependence on fossil fuels.

2. **In order for a society to be sustainable, nature's functions and diversity are not systematically subject to increasing concentrations of substances produced by society.**

In a sustainable society, humans will avoid generating systematic increases in persistent substances such as DDT, PCBs, and freon. Synthetic organic compounds such as DDT and PCBs can remain in the environment for many years, bioaccumulating in the tissue of organisms, causing profound deleterious effects on predators in the upper levels of the food chain. Freon, and other ozone depleting compounds, may increase risk of cancer due to added UV radiation in the troposphere. Society needs to find ways to reduce economic dependence on persistent human-made substances.

3. **In order for a society to be sustainable, nature's functions and diversity are not systematically impoverished by physical displacement, over-harvesting or other forms of ecosystem manipulation.**

In a sustainable society, humans will avoid taking more from the biosphere than can be replenished by natural systems. In addition, people will avoid systematically encroaching upon nature by destroying the habitat of other species. Biodiversity, which includes the great variety of animals and plants found in nature, provides the foundation for ecosystem services which are necessary to sustain life on this planet. Society's health and prosperity depend on the enduring capacity of nature to renew itself and rebuild waste into resources.

4. In a sustainable society resources are used fairly and efficiently in order to meet basic human needs globally.

Meeting the fourth system condition is a way to avoid violating the first three system conditions for sustainability. Considering the human enterprise as a whole, we need to be efficient with regard to resource use and waste generation in order to be sustainable. If one billion people lack adequate nutrition while another billion have more than they need, there is a lack of fairness with regard to meeting basic human needs. Achieving greater fairness is essential for social stability and the cooperation needed for making large-scale changes within the framework laid out by the first three conditions.

To achieve this fourth condition, humanity must strive to improve technical and organizational efficiency around the world, and to live using fewer resources, especially in affluent areas. System condition number four implies an improved means of addressing human population growth. If the total resource throughput of the global human population continues to increase, it will be increasingly difficult to meet basic human needs as human-driven processes intended to fulfill human needs and wants are systematically degrading the collective capacity of the earth's ecosystems to meet these demands.

One of the strengths of the Natural Step lies in its scientifically based framework, which supports measurable results based on the laws of thermodynamics and natural cycles.[22] System Condition 1 explains why the extraction of fossil fuels and other minerals must not increase their concentration in the ecosphere. This condition ties into the First Law of Thermodynamics, which states that total mass and energy in the universe is conserved. For example, the burning of fossil fuels simply creates gases in the atmosphere. The corrective action for System Condition 1 encourages us to "implement comprehensive metal and mineral recycling programs, and decrease economic dependence on fossil fuels."

System Condition 2 describes how human-generated substances such as DDT and PCBs damage species through the food chain and compounds such as freon deplete the ozone. This system condition is based on the Second Law of Thermodynamics (the Law of Entropy), in which energy and matter tend to spread spontaneously and everything has a tendency to disperse.[23] System Condition 2, which challenges us to "find ways to reduce economic dependence on persistent human-made substances," highlights bioaccumulation, whereby substances that are absorbed into ecosystems and progress through the food web with increasing concentration are potentially harmful to species, including humans. Examples range from mercury and lead poisoning to water pollution and toxic waste.

Maintaining the integrity of ecosystems, including species biodiversity, is underscored by System Condition 3.[24] Species, habitats and natural resources must not be "systematically impoverished" through "physical displacement, over-harvesting" and other practices. This system condition emphasizes the need to value the functions of living systems, including water and air purification, pollination and climate regulation, and to allow for their renewal through sustainable methods of agriculture, forestry, fishing and urban growth. System Condition 3 calls for a "systems thinking" approach to resource management and biological conservation. By understanding the value of the relationships in an ecosystem rather than merely its components, we will be better positioned to make wise decisions.

Finally, System Condition 4 speaks to the issue of equity. This condition, though not scientifically based, provides an essential ethical aspect to the Natural Step. The condition calls for fair and efficient use of resources, "essential for social stability and the cooperation needed for making large-scale changes within the framework laid out by the first three conditions." Thus, System Condition 4 gives meaning to System Conditions 1, 2 and 3 by seeking an equitable distribution of resources from more affluent areas to poorer ones and "improved means of addressing human population growth." The population issue is a very complex and critical one. Although the Natural Step suggests no specific solutions, a more even distribution of resources lays the foundation for tackling the population problem.

The scientific basis of the Natural Step lends it legitimacy within the business community. Working closely with businesses, the Natural Step provides tools such as ecological auditing, "backcasting" and systems-thinking methods that businesses can adapt for developing sustainable practices. Companies and institutions such as Ikea, Interface, Scandic Hotels AB and the University of Texas at Houston have implemented the Natural Step in their business practices.[25]

The Natural Step utilizes compelling graphics to emphasize the conflict between consumption and resource availability. The dilemma is illustrated using a funnel where demand for resources is one wall and resource availability is the other.[26] As aggregate demand increases and capacity to meet the demand decreases, we are moving as a society into the narrower portion of the funnel. The funnel metaphor presents sustainability issues to the business community in a simple and powerful style.

The Natural Step's framework also can be used in mid- and small-sized businesses and in educational institutions from high schools through universities. In fact, because of the educational community's academic background in science, business, economics and ethics, it may be one of the most successful arenas for promoting the Natural Step.

The Natural Step effectively blends knowledge of scientific laws with management practices to create a dynamic sustainability model for businesses and institutions. The Natural Step's rapid success in Europe is perhaps due to the historically close working relationship between the business community and the government agencies that have assisted in the Natural Step's implementation. In the US, however, the business sector's traditional wariness of government involvement may be limiting the Natural Step's widespread adoption.

The Houston Principles

The Natural Step's melding of management and science is paralleled by the linking of the labor and environmental movements in the Houston Principles. The Houston Principles represent one of the hallmarks of the Sustainability Revolution: the alliance of seemingly disparate interest groups (the labor and environmental movements) with a common objective (corporate accountability and social responsibility). The Houston Principles bring to the forefront a new holistic perspective that calls for corporate accountability to employees, the environment and the livelihood of the communities where business is done.

The Houston Principles arose in 1999 from the opposition by the Alliance for Sustainable Jobs and the Environment to the clear-cutting of ancient redwoods in Northern California by the Pacific Lumber Company, owned by Maxxam Corporation. The Alliance for Sustainable Jobs and the Environment is a coalition of environmental and labor groups committed to holding corporations such as Maxxam accountable for their "impact on working people, communities, and the environment."[27]

Houston principles of the alliance for sustainable jobs and the environment[28]

Preamble:

On May 19, 1999, environmental and labor leaders confronted CEO Charles Hurwitz in Houston to demand that his Maxxam Corporation, which owns Kaiser Aluminum and Pacific Lumber Company, be held accountable for its impact on working people, communities and the environment.

By clear-cutting ancient redwoods in Northern California, and by locking-out striking steelworkers in five cities, the Maxxam Corporation has become an icon of corporate irresponsibility.

Recognizing that we have a common interest in making corporations more accountable for their behavior world-wide, environmental and labor leaders have formed the Alliance for Sustainable Jobs and the Environment and circulated the following statement, dubbed the "Houston Principles."

Whereas:

The spectacular accumulation of wealth by corporations and America's most affluent during the past two decades has come with a huge price tag.

Corporations have become more powerful than the government entities designed to regulate them.

The goal of a giant, global corporation is to maximize wealth and to wield political power on its own behalf. Too often, corporate leaders regard working people, communities, and the natural world as resources to be used and thrown away.

Recognizing the tremendous stakes, labor unions and environmental advocates are beginning to recognize our common ground. Together we can challenge illegitimate corporate authority over our country's and communities' governing decisions.

While we may not agree on everything, we are determined to accelerate our efforts to make alliances as often as possible.

We believe that:

A healthy future for the economy and the environment requires a dynamic alliance between labor, management, and environmental advocates.

The same forces that threaten economic and biological sustainability undermine the democratic process.

The drive for short-term profits without regard for long-term sustainability hurts working people, communities, and the earth.

Labor, environmental and community groups need to take action to organize as a counter-balance to abusive corporate power.

The environmental and labor advocates who have signed these principles resolve to work together to:
Remind the public that the original purpose behind the creation of corporations was to serve the public interest — namely working people, communities, and the earth.

Seek stricter enforcement of labor laws and advocate for new laws to guarantee working people their right to form unions and their right to bargain collectively.

Make workplaces, communities and the planet safer by reducing waste and greenhouse gas emissions.

Demand that global trade agreements include enforceable labor and environmental standards.

Promote forward-thinking business models that allow for sustainability over the long term while protecting working people, communities, and the environment.

This ground-breaking alliance of labor and environmentalists invites all people to join with us in a spirit of creative cooperation. Together, we can forge a partnership that protects people and the planet.

The Houston Principles are the result of a powerful alliance between the labor and environmental movements, which historically have been at odds. As the document points out: "A healthy future for the economy and the environment requires a dynamic alliance between labor, management, and environmental advocates."

The Houston Principles highlight the interdependence of ecological, economic and equity issues — the Three Es of sustainability — illustrating a convergence of concerns that previously have divided labor and environmental groups. The labor movement's advocacy of jobs is now linked to the environmentalists' fight for healthy ecosystems. Because the "drive for short-term profits without regard for long-term sustainability hurts working people, communities, and the earth," the two groups have banded together to "challenge illegitimate corporate authority over our country's and communities' governing decisions."

The Houston Principles call for a shift from corporate power, where decisions often are made in boardrooms by executives living in different states or countries, to local involvement in determining the fate of a community. This grievance is as much about the impact of these decisions as about the decision-making process, which undercuts the democratic rights of citizens. The Alliance for Sustainable Jobs and the Environment is committed to "organize as a counter-balance to abusive corporate power."

One of the strengths of the Houston Principles lies in outlining a strategic process for implementing its goals, which include: (1) enforcing of labor laws and the ability to form unions and practice collective bargaining; (2) reducing waste and greenhouse gases; (3) enforcing labor and environmental standards in international trade agreements; and (4) promoting business models that support sustainability values.

The Houston Principles support accountability for companies and organizations that reduce jobs and livelihoods in pursuit of profits. International agencies such as the World Trade Organization (WTO) and the International Monetary Fund (IMF) are primary targets of the Houston Principles because their practices often disrupt the viability of local economies. The large public demonstrations at the WTO Conference in Seattle in 1999 and the IMF Conference in Washington, DC, in 2000 showed that the combined force of the labor and environmental movements is formidable. These agencies and the international community have begun to recognize the concerns of workers and environmentalists.

The CERES Principles

The Houston Principles' call for corporate accountability is echoed in a less confrontational fashion in the CERES Principles, which provide a framework for organizations' sustainability practices. The CERES Principles give large, medium-sized and small companies a means to adopt sustainable practices in a low-risk, safe and supportive setting. CERES assists institutions to evaluate their environmental and social performance at their own pace and in a completely voluntary manner. Though some critics may scoff at the environmental record of multinational CERES endorsers including General Motors, ITT Industries and Bank of America, the impact of CERES lies in promoting public accountability and encouraging the public disclosure of environmental performance and socially responsible initiatives from a wide range of institutions.

The CERES Principles, formerly known as the Valdez Principles, evolved from the environmental disaster caused by the 1989 Exxon Valdez oil spill in Alaska. As a nonprofit organization advocating corporate environmental responsibility, CERES is made up of a coalition of over 80 investor, environmental, religious, labor and social justice groups and over 70 corporate endorsers from various industries, including several Fortune 500 firms.[29]

The CERES Principles establish a forum for sustainability in the business community. They provide a standard for corporations to meet in their environmental reporting and a model of cooperation for evaluating managerial styles and adopting sustainable management practices. As stated in the document: "These Principles establish an environmental ethic with criteria by which investors and others can assess the environmental performance of companies."

An important aspect of the CERES Principles is that response from participating members is voluntary. Rather than requiring legal compliance, CERES establishes a dialogue and works with organizations to meet measurable sustainability goals. Using self-evaluations and environmental audits, members complete the CERES report, which is made available to the public.

The CERES principles[30]

Endorsing Company Statement

By adopting these Principles, we publicly affirm our belief that corporations have a responsibility for the environment, and must conduct all aspects of their business as responsible stewards of the environment by operating in a manner that protects the Earth. We believe that corporations must not compromise the ability of future generations to sustain themselves.

We will update our practices constantly in light of advances in technology and new understandings in health and environmental science. In collaboration with CERES, we will promote a dynamic process to ensure that the Principles are interpreted in a way that accommodates changing technologies and environmental realities. We intend to make consistent, measurable progress in implementing these Principles and to apply them to all aspects of our operations throughout the world.

Principles

Protection of the Biosphere

We will reduce and make continual progress toward eliminating the release of any substance that may cause environmental damage to the air, water, or the earth or its inhabitants. We will safeguard all habitats affected by our operations and will protect open spaces and wilderness, while preserving biodiversity.

Sustainable Use of Natural Resources

We will make sustainable use of renewable natural resources, such as water, soils and forests. We will conserve non-renewable natural resources through efficient use and careful planning.

Reduction and Disposal of Wastes

We will reduce and where possible eliminate waste through source reduction and recycling. All waste will be handled and disposed of through safe and responsible methods.

Energy Conservation

We will conserve energy and improve the energy efficiency of our internal operations and of the goods and services we sell. We will make every effort to use environmentally safe and sustainable energy sources.

Risk Reduction

We will strive to minimize the environmental, health and safety risks to our employees and the communities in which we operate through safe technologies, facilities and operating procedures, and by being prepared for emergencies.

Safe Products and Services

We will reduce and where possible eliminate the use, manufacture or sale of products and services that cause environmental damage or health or safety hazards. We will inform our customers of the environmental impacts of our products or services and try to correct unsafe use.

Environmental Restoration

We will promptly and responsibly correct conditions we have caused that endanger health, safety or the environment. To the extent feasible, we will redress injuries we have caused to persons or damage we have caused to the environment and will restore the environment.

Informing the Public

We will inform in a timely manner everyone who may be affected by conditions caused by our company that might endanger health, safety or the environment. We will regularly seek advice and counsel through dialogue with persons in communities near our facilities. We will not take any action against employees for reporting dangerous incidents or conditions to management or to appropriate authorities.

Management Commitment

We will implement these Principles and sustain a process that ensures that the Board of Directors and Chief Executive Officer are fully informed about pertinent environmental issues and are fully responsible for environmental policy. In selecting our Board of Directors, we will consider demonstrated environmental commitment as a factor.

Audits and Reports

We will conduct an annual self-evaluation of our progress in implementing these Principles. We will support the timely creation of generally accepted environmental audit procedures. We will annually complete the CERES Report, which will be made available to the public.

Disclaimer

These Principles establish an environmental ethic with criteria by which investors and others can assess the environmental performance of companies. Companies that endorse these Principles pledge to go voluntarily beyond the requirements of the law. The terms "may" and "might" in Principles one and eight are not meant to encompass every imaginable consequence, no matter how remote. Rather, these Principles obligate endorsers to behave as prudent persons who are not governed by conflicting interests and who possess a strong commitment to environmental excellence and to human health and safety. These Principles are not intended to create new legal liabilities, expand existing rights or obligations, waive legal defenses, or otherwise affect the legal position of any endorsing company, and are not intended to be used against an endorser in any legal proceeding for any purpose.

The CERES Principles cover many of the areas mentioned in the other frameworks, including protection of the biosphere, energy conservation, environmental restoration, waste reduction and sustainable use of resources. However, these principles also focus on issues of primary concern to employees such as personal health and safety. The Risk Reduction clause, for example, stipulates that CERES members will "minimize the environmental, health and safety risks to our employees and the communities in which we operate." This phrase highlights the need for corporate responsibility to the local community and the well-being of every employee. Tied to the commitment to risk reduction is public notification. CERES members agree to inform the public in a timely manner of any activities that "might endanger health, safety, or the environment."

Although most current business practices and the "business as usual" approach have had a negative impact on the environment and on local communities, the CERES Principles provide a model for companies to use to assess this impact.

The ICC Charter and ISO 14000

Together with CERES, the International Chamber of Commerce's (ICC) Business Charter for Sustainable Development is having an important international impact in expanding the number of organizations embracing sustainable practices. In addition, the International Standard Organization's (ISO) 14000 family of international standards for management provides a useful and widely recognized mechanism to measure environmental progress. Whereas the ICC principles outline an internationally recognized approach to sustainability, ISO 14000 provides the tools necessary to implement the goals and objectives.

The significance of the ICC's charter comes from its thousands of member companies and associations from over 130 countries.[31] Although the charter lacks assessment mechanisms, it provides useful guidelines for organizations striving for sustainable practices. The ISO 14000 family of standards, including ISO 14001, ISO 14004 and ISO 14031, focuses on environmental management systems and tools to assist an organization in "realizing its environmental policy objectives and targets."[32]

Environmental Assessments and Green Taxes

Two additional tools, environmental assessments and green taxes, have the potential for dramatically increasing the sustainability of business practices. The discussion and implementation of environmental assessments and green taxes, including "tax shifting," have had a positive impact on the debate about corporate responsibility in the commercial sector.

Environmental assessments, which are followed by ecological audits, assist businesses with quantifying their environmental impacts in areas such as energy, waste, toxics and land use. After assessment of a firm's operations, a plan with measurable goals and objectives is implemented to reduce impacts and increase savings. The benefits of ecological audits are easily understood by large companies with big budgets, progressive outlooks and acceptance of long-term payback. It still is difficult to convince small businesses and organizations of the long-term benefits of these services.

"Tax shifting" (green taxes) provides a means to restructure the tax code to reduce or eliminate payroll, sales, property and personal income taxes. Taxes shift to activities — many currently subsidized by government — that cause environmental harm such as greenhouse gases, air and water pollution and traffic congestion. In essence, the government shifts taxes from what we want more of (income, payroll) to what we want less of (pollution, waste).

At present, Europe leads in adopting tax-shifting strategies. Sweden taxes carbon-based fuels and carbon dioxide emissions. France, Germany and the Netherlands use a tax on water pollution to build wastewater treatment plants. Denmark taxes pesticides and herbicides. Switzerland taxes volatile organic compounds (VOCs) to reduce ground-level ozone and Great Britain uses a landfill tax to reduce assessments on payrolls.[33] In the US more than twenty states have developed tax-shifting plans for controlling greenhouse gases including carbon dioxide. Vermont, Minnesota and Oregon are at the forefront of implementing these initiatives.

As Alan Durning, former researcher at Worldwatch Institute and executive director of Northwest Environment Watch, points out:

> Shifting the tax burden would send out powerful signals
> — signals that would re-orient consumption and
> production in our homes and businesses. Tax shifting
> would harness the profit motive for environmental
> ends and wring out the waste of resources.

Governments would still get their money, and —
because taxes on "bads" do not bog down the
economy as much as many existing taxes on "goods"
— employment levels and incomes would rise.[34]

Environmental assessments and tax shifting are powerful incentives toward sustainable business practices. Although both tools have proven themselves, further education about their advantages will increase acceptance and adoption.

A New Business Model

The Sustainability Revolution is challenging business managers to reevaluate how they operate their enterprises and how they measure success. Their focus is shifting from environmental compliance to ecological, economic and social responsibility. Corporate leaders are aware that measuring success involves delivering value and being accountable to their employees, their customers and the communities in which they operate.

> **The Sustainability Revolution is challenging business managers to reevaluate how they operate their enterprises and how they measure success.**

The Precautionary, Natural Step, Houston and CERES Principles are blazing the way toward a new business model that strives to understand and emulate natural systems while maintaining a thriving economic and social agenda. The ecological, economic and equity components of sustainability are no longer viewed as competing but rather as complementary. The choice is not economic growth at the expense of the environment but environmental protection, a vibrant economy and equitable resource distribution.

CHAPTER 4

Sustainability and
Natural Resources

*It's bizarre that the produce manager is more important
to my children's health than the pediatrician.*

—Meryl Streep

*Destroying rainforest for economic gain is like burning a
Renaissance painting to cook a meal.*

—E.O. Wilson

The Contradictions of Resource Extraction

THE RESOURCE EXTRACTION INDUSTRIES, including petroleum, lumber, fisheries and agriculture, highlight the challenges of devising sustainable strategies for activities that have a direct impact on the Earth. Today the same industries that helped build the foundation for the Industrial Revolution are retooling and seeking alternative ways to manage their operations.

The Sustainability and Natural Resources principles reflect the challenges faced by industries that attempt to implement sustainable practices while depending directly on the Earth's natural resources for their survival. This situation presents a series of conflicting interests. Unlike industries that rely on processed goods, resource extraction industries are directly responsible for obtaining and managing primary resources including minerals, oil and gas, timber, fish and land for agriculture. Traditionally, humans managed to harvest these resources in a sustainable fashion. However, in the industrial and post-industrial period we have dramatically increased our appetite for resources, plunging many of the world's ecosystems into decline.

In evaluating the sustainability aspects of the natural resources principles, two key variables stand out: (1) resource renewal versus nonrenewal and (2) short-term versus long-term perspective. The first calls for assessing whether the resource is renewable or not. In the case of nonrenewable fossil fuels and minerals, for example, it is a daunting challenge for industries to claim sustainable practices. Sustainability of nonrenewable resources requires recycling of existing materials and shifting to renewable alternatives. In the case of renewable resources, industries must devise sustainable practices while remaining competitive.

The time perspective factor highlights the tendency for industries to focus on short-term profits, which in the extraction industries often results in destruction of resources. Long-term perspectives, which are compatible with sustainable practices, require a comprehensive strategy that minimizes the impact of market-driven economic pressures by adopting an extended time period for desired results.

Many of the principles in Sustainability and Natural Resources claim to value the integrity of the land and its resources. However, the actions of the mining, lumber, fishing, agribusiness and other industries point to a significant credibility gap. The track record of many of these industries contradicts the intentions expressed in their principles.

Although the principles mention concerns about biodiversity and ecological health (the First E), these industries' actions, now beyond the preservation phase, still do not emphasize the need to repair and restore the damage already done. The need to search for and develop alternative renewable sources of energy also is omitted from these principles. Activities such as oil drilling, clearcutting, overfishing and industrial farming historically have destroyed the environment. Recognition of the environmental damage done and renewed attention to sustainable approaches and ecological restoration would instill a refreshing policy direction.

In Sustainability and Natural Resources we will focus on principles from industries with a direct impact on environmental resources, namely: petroleum, lumber, fisheries and agriculture. We will examine the American Petroleum Institute's (API) Environmental, Health and Safety Principles, which represent a segment of the energy industry concerned with oil and natural gas extraction and refining; the Forest Stewardship Council's (FSC) Principles and Criteria of Forest Stewardship; the Marine Stewardship Council's (MSC) Principles and Criteria for Sustainable Fishing; and the Alliance for Sustainability's Seven Challenges for the agricultural industry.

The API principles focus primarily on the safety and operational aspects of the oil industry, including facility operations, manufacturing processes and waste management. The FSC principles take a comprehensive approach to wood harvesting practices and their relationship to ecosystems and local communities. The MSC principles highlight the global issues concerning fisheries management and conservation. Finally, the Alliance for Sustainability's Seven Challenges underscore the tremendous impact of agribusiness on family farms and local communities and call for the establishment of sustainable farming practices.

American Petroleum Institute (API) Environmental, Health and Safety Principles

The API principles aim to continue existing extraction practices while attempting to safeguard the environment. According to its mission statement, API members pledge "to influence public policy in support of a strong, viable US oil and natural gas industry essential to meet the energy needs of consumers in an efficient, environmentally responsible manner."

This clause highlights a key challenge for the oil industry: continuously juggling the delicate balance between environmental protection and resource extraction. The effects of oil spills and drilling operations often have a high public profile and are devastating to the environment. Companies in the oil industry attempt to reconcile this fundamental incompatibility by (a) promoting the need for fossil fuels for economic growth and (b) projecting a caring attitude toward the environment through public relations campaigns.

As a Washington, DC-based trade association with over 400 members, API represents "all segments of the industry... producers, refiners, suppliers, pipeline operators and marine transporters."[1] API was first established in 1919 to set standards for drilling and production equipment. Presently, API is responsible for public policy concerns affecting the industry.

American Petroleum Institute environmental, health and safety principles [2]

The members of the American Petroleum Institute are dedicated to continuous efforts to improve the compatibility of their operations with the environment while economically developing energy resources and supplying high quality products and services to consumers.

Our members recognize their responsibility to work with the public, the government, and others to develop and to use natural resources in an environmentally sound manner while protecting the health and safety of our employees and the public.

To meet these responsibilities, API members pledge to manage their businesses according to the following principles, using sound science to prioritize risks and to implement cost-effective management practices:

To recognize and to respond to community concerns about our raw materials, products and operations.

To operate our plants and facilities and to handle our raw materials and products in a manner that protects the environment and the safety and health of our employees and the public.

To make safety, health and environmental considerations a priority in our planning and our development of new products and processes.

To advise promptly appropriate officials, employees, customers and the public of information on significant industry-related safety, health and environmental hazards, and to recommend protective measures.

To counsel customers, transporters and others in the safe use, transportation and disposal of our raw materials, products and waste materials.

To economically develop and produce natural resources and to conserve those resources by using energy efficiently.

To extend knowledge by conducting or supporting research on the safety, health and environmental effects of our raw materials, products, processes and waste materials.

To commit to reduce overall emission and waste generation.

To work with others to resolve problems created by handling and disposal of hazardous substances from our operations.

To participate with government and others in creating responsible laws, regulations and standards to safeguard the community, workplace and environment.

To promote these principles and practices by sharing experiences and offering assistance to others who produce, handle, use, transport or dispose of similar raw materials, petroleum products and wastes.

The safety and health concerns emphasized in the API principles underscore the dangers for those manufacturing petroleum products and for people living near refineries. The principles aim to "make safety, health, and environmental considerations a priority in our planning, and our development of new products and processes." The safety message illustrates the industry's efforts to improve its poor track record marked by public concern over refinery accidents, oil spills and related incidents. The repercussions from legal actions are a motivating factor for stressing safety, health and environmental protection. Companies in the oil industry are responsible for mandated compliance standards and susceptible to lawsuits from employees working at refineries and residents of neighboring communities.

The safe disposal of waste materials and waste reduction are other key factors addressed by the API principles. The disposal issue covers the safe handling and disposal of hazardous substances, particularly relevant to oil refineries and other manufacturing plants dealing with toxic waste products. In addition, API calls for the reduction of overall emissions and of waste generation. The API principles also loosely promote the conservation of resources, asking members to "economically develop and produce natural resources and to conserve those resources by using energy efficiently."

One of the essential elements missing from the API principles is a strong call for a reduction of energy consumption and a shift away from fossil fuels to renewable energy sources. The world's limited supply of petroleum and declining production forecasts make the shift to renewable energy a logical trend. Nevertheless, the focus of the industry remains on extraction and production practices. The API principles emphasize the management and operations of the manufacturing processes. The principles cover the safety and disposal of raw materials and products and promote "responsible laws, regulations and standards to safeguard the community, workplace and environment."

The concept of equity also is absent from the API principles. The equitable distribution of resources to those in need is overlooked. In addition, the voluntary adoption of the principles by API members leaves no room for the accountability and progress reports of the member organizations. In essence, the API principles provide a statement with a limited perspective on the industry's impact and responsibility to society.

Forest Stewardship Council (FSC) Principles and Criteria of Forest Stewardship

While the oil industry seeks to promote sustainable use of a nonrenewable resource, the lumber industry attempts to implement sustainable use of a renewable resource. The Forest Stewardship Council was founded in 1993 as an independent international non-profit organization "to promote environmentally appropriate, socially beneficial and economically viable management of the world's forests." Although there are several forest certification systems, including the American Tree Farm System, Canadian Standards Association (CSA) International and Sustainable Forestry International (SFI),[3] FSC is rapidly setting a global standard for sustainable forest management practices, with 42 million hectares certified in over 60 countries. Thousands of products worldwide are made using FSC-certified wood.[4]

The 10 FSC principles and 57 criteria apply to all FSC-certified forests worldwide and address issues such as respecting applicable laws, indigenous and workers' rights, environmental impact and creating a management plan and monitoring system. The FSC principles also emphasize improving the relationship of the logging industry with its employees and with local communities. This attitude stands in contrast to a predominant group of transnational corporations that have neglected the role of local communities in the decision-making process.[5]

Forest stewardship council principles[6]

Principle 1: Compliance with Laws and FSC Principles
Forest management shall respect all applicable laws of the country in which they occur, and international treaties and agreements to which the country is a signatory, and comply with all FSC Principles and Criteria.

Principle 2: Tenure and Use Rights and Responsibilities
Long-term tenure and use rights to the land and forest resources shall be clearly defined, documented and legally established.

Principle 3: Indigenous Peoples' Rights
The legal and customary rights of indigenous peoples to own, use and manage their lands, territories, and resources shall be recognized and respected.

Principle 4: Community Relations and Workers' Rights
Forest management operations shall maintain or enhance the long-term social and economic well-being of forest workers and local communities.

Principle 5: Benefits from the Forest
Forest management operations shall encourage the efficient use of the forest's multiple products and services to ensure economic viability and a wide range of environmental and social benefits.

Principle 6: Environmental Impact
Forest management shall conserve biological diversity and its associated values, water resources, soils, and unique and fragile ecosystems and landscapes, and, by so doing, maintain the ecological functions and the integrity of the forest.

Principle 7: Management Plan
A management plan — appropriate to the scale and intensity of the operations — shall be written, implemented, and kept up to date. The long term objectives of management, and the means of achieving them, shall be clearly stated.

Principle 8: Monitoring and Assessment
Monitoring shall be conducted — appropriate to the scale and intensity of forest management — to assess the condition of the forest, yields of forest products, chain of custody, management activities and their social and environmental impacts.

Principle 9: Maintenance of High Conservation Value Forests
Management activities in high conservation value forests shall maintain or enhance the attributes which define such forests. Decisions regarding high conservation value

forests shall always be considered in the context of a precautionary approach.

Principle 10: Plantations
Plantations shall be planned and managed in accordance with Principles and Criteria 1–9, and Principle 10 and its Criteria. While plantations can provide an array of social and economic benefits, and can contribute to satisfying the world's needs for forest products, they should complement the management of, reduce pressures on, and promote the restoration and conservation of natural forests.

The FSC principles focus on promoting sustainable forest practices by ensuring that forest management "shall conserve biological diversity and its associated values, water resources, soils, and unique and fragile ecosystems and landscapes, and, by so doing, maintain the ecological functions and the integrity of the forest." The principles also call for protecting the rights of indigenous peoples and instituting efficient forest management practices "to ensure economic viability and a wide range of environmental and social benefits." These phrases emphasize the significance of balancing ecosystem health with indigenous rights and social benefits for workers.

The FSC principles ensure an integrated forest management approach with tracking and accountability mechanisms. FSC-certified forests require owners to maintain an updated management plan with clearly stated long-term objectives. Moreover, the credibility of the FSC label is assured by the "chain of custody" process whereby any FSC product can be traced back to its original FSC-certified forest. This link between the final product and its source assures customers that the wood comes from a forest managed according to FSC standards.

In contrast to the American Petroleum Institute's principles, the FSC principles wrestle with the issues of equity and employment by promoting the role of indigenous peoples and local communities in the decisions made by logging companies, illustrating a commitment to the people dependent on the company for their livelihood.

These principles provide a vision for maintaining logging jobs as well as the health of the forest, affirming that through wise management economic vitality and sustainable forest practices can coexist. In addition, the principles provide a rigorous third-party monitoring mechanism to maintain members' adherence to FSC standards.

The FSC principles specifically address the management of "high conservation value forests" by requiring "a precautionary approach." The precautionary principle's call for thorough investigation before any action plays a critical role in managing particularly sensitive areas, old growth and forests high in species biodiversity. In addition, plantations, which often severely undermine the biodiversity of an ecosystem, "should complement the management of, reduce pressures on, and promote the restoration and conservation of natural forests."

As an encouraging sign of the success of the FSC principles, with added pressure from environmental groups several large retailers including Home Depot (which claims to be the largest lumber retailer in the world), Lowe's and Andersen have agreed to sell certified wood when it is available.[7] In 2003 Boise Cascade Corporation became the largest American forest products company to completely eliminate the purchase of wood from endangered areas. With a policy that extends to Boise's US and international operations and to all of its suppliers, this is a landmark decision for the industry.[8]

Marine Stewardship Council (MSC) Principles and Criteria for Sustainable Fishing[9]

The Marine Stewardship Council's Principles and Criteria for Sustainable Fishing demonstrate that many of the concerns expressed in the Forest Stewardship Council principles are made more complex by the international and dynamic nature of the fisheries industry. Approximately a billion people worldwide rely on fish as their primary source of protein.[10] This tremendous dependence on our oceans has resulted in a fivefold increase in the world's oceanic fish catch from 19 million tons in 1950 to over 90 million tons in 1997, a stark reminder that we have surpassed the catch limit.[11]

Devising an effective set of principles addressing sustainable fishing practices has been a difficult assignment for the fishing industry, international organizations and governments attempting to maintain the viability of the world's fish stocks. Fishing fleets often operate in international waters, searching for a resource that knows no boundaries.

As an independent nonprofit organization established in 1999 by the World Wildlife Fund (WWF) and Unilever (the world's largest seafood buying company), the Marine Stewardship Council aims to "enhance responsible management of seafood resources [and] to ensure the sustainability of global fish stocks and the health of the marine ecosystem."[12] As an alliance of a nonprofit (WWF) and a for-profit (Unilever), the MSC is an encouraging model for future cooperation between these two sectors.

The Marine Stewardship Council's principles grew out of the Food and Agriculture Organization's (FAO) Code of Conduct for Responsible Fisheries.[13] Similar to the Forest Stewardship Council in structure, the MSC provides a third-party certification process, including accreditation and chain of custody procedures, that identifies sustainably harvested seafood products through its eco-label, the MSC logo. The MSC certification process is rapidly gaining global acceptance, with ten certified fisheries and suppliers, including the Alaskan salmon, New Zealand hoki, Thames herring and the Mexican Baja California red rock lobster. For shoppers interested in sustainably harvested fish, there are almost 200 MSC-labeled seafood products in fourteen countries.[14]

MSC principles[15]
Preamble
The following Principles and Criteria are intended to guide the efforts of the Marine Stewardship Council towards the development of sustainable fisheries on a global basis. They were developed assuming that a sustainable fishery is defined, for the purposes of MSC certification, as one that is conducted in such a way that:

- it can be continued indefinitely at a reasonable level;
- it maintains, and seeks to maximise, ecological health and abundance;
- it maintains the diversity, structure and function of the ecosystem on which it depends as well as the quality of its habitat, minimising the adverse effects that it causes;
- it is managed and operated in a responsible manner, in conformity with local, national and international laws and regulations;
- it maintains present and future economic and social options and benefits;
- it is conducted in a socially and economically fair and responsible manner.

The Principles represent the overarching philosophical basis for this initiative in stewardship of marine resources: the use of market forces to promote behaviour which helps achieve the goal of sustainable fisheries. They form the basis for detailed Criteria which will be used to evaluate each fishery seeking certification under the MSC programme. Although the primary focus is the ecological integrity of world fisheries, the principles also embrace the human and social elements of fisheries. Their successful implementation depends upon a system which is open, fair, based upon the best information available and which incorporates all relevant legal obligations. The certification programme in which these principles will be applied is intended to give any fishery the opportunity to demonstrate its commitment to sustainable fishing and ultimately benefit from this commitment in the market place.

Scope
The scope of the MSC Principles and Criteria relates to marine fisheries activities up to but not beyond the point at which the fish are landed. However, MSC-accredited certi-

fiers may be informed of serious concerns associated with post-landing practices.

The MSC Principles and Criteria apply at this stage only to wildcapture fisheries (including, but not limited to, shell-fish, crustaceans and cephalopods). Aquaculture and the harvest of other species are not currently included.

Issues involving allocation of quotas and access to marine resources are considered to be beyond the scope of these Principles and Criteria.

Principle 1:
A fishery must be conducted in a manner that does not lead to over-fishing or depletion of the exploited populations and, for those populations that are depleted, the fishery must be conducted in a manner that demonstrably leads to their recovery:

Intent:
The intent of this principle is to ensure that the productive capacities of resources are maintained at high levels and are not sacrificed in favour of short term interests. Thus, exploited populations would be maintained at high levels of abundance designed to retain their productivity, provide margins of safety for error and uncertainty, and restore and retain their capacities for yields over the long term.

Principle 2:
Fishing operations should allow for the maintenance of the structure, productivity, function and diversity of the ecosystem (including habitat and associated dependent and ecologically related species) on which the fishery depends.

Intent:
The intent of this principle is to encourage the management of fisheries from an ecosystem perspective under a system designed to assess and restrain the impacts of the fishery on the ecosystem.

Principle 3:
The fishery is subject to an effective management system that respects local, national and international laws and standards and incorporates institutional and operational frameworks that require use of the resource to be responsible and sustainable.

Intent:
The intent of this principle is to ensure that there is an institutional and operational framework for implementing Principles 1 and 2, appropriate to the size and scale of the fishery.

One of the interesting points raised by the Marine Stewardship Council principles involves a systems approach for promoting not merely the conservation of a specific species but the "maintenance of the structure, productivity, function and diversity of the ecosystem (including habitat and associated dependent and ecologically related species) on which the fishery depends." This approach emphasizes the interdependence of all living organisms within an ecosystem.

The MSC principles also support a "management system that respects local, national and international laws and standards" as a mechanism for implementing sustainable fishing practices. One of the challenges that arise from international trade agreements such as the WTO is that local economies from developing countries are subject to the unpredictable prices of the international marketplace and lose control of their local resources. Although industrial countries account for over 80 percent of all fish imports, developing countries are providing an increasing percentage of the exports (37 percent in 1970 and 49 percent by 1997).[16]

International fisheries consumption also is having a devastating effect on fish stocks. In the last 50 years, 90 percent of all large ocean predators — tuna, marlin, swordfish, sharks, cod, halibut, skates and flounder — have been fished out by industrial fleets.[17] WTO policies have been found to be in conflict with national environmental protection measures, as in the case of the sea turtles (protected under US law) caught by shrimp fishing fleets.[18]

The MSC principles also include the precautionary principle in the management system criteria section, which calls for organizations to "act in a timely and adaptive fashion on the basis of the best available information using a precautionary approach particularly when dealing with scientific uncertainty."[19] The MSC principles would, for example, require a fishing moratorium when there is inconclusive scientific data regarding the viability of fish stocks. This "better safe than sorry" approach is particularly challenging to enforce when so much of the world's population depends on fish. Nevertheless, this perspective would protect against potential devastating effects of overfishing, which already have been experienced in many regions of the world.

Perhaps the fast adoption of the MSC principles is due in part to its limited yet well-defined scope. The principles focus primarily on the ecological aspects of the fishing industry and to a much lesser degree on the social aspects. In addition, the principles concentrate on wildcapture fisheries and do not encompass aquaculture and other harvested species. The strength of these principles lies in their focus and effective implementation mechanisms.

Finally, the MSC principles include a temporal perspective, vowing to ensure that "productive capacities of resources are maintained at high levels and are not sacrificed in favour of short term interests." Achieving this long-term goal includes setting catch levels, using fishing methods that protect habitats (such as no use of poisons or explosives) and establishing "no take zones."

The Asilomar Declaration for Sustainable Agriculture

Many of the issues raised by the Marine Stewardship Council principles confront the sustainable agriculture community in its quest to survive the impact of agribusiness. The Asilomar Declaration represents an effort to establish sustainable farming in the mainstream of society.

The Asilomar Declaration's Seven Challenges call for promoting sustainable agriculture through increased education and participation by government agencies and by educational and international institutions. The declaration questions the benefits of the global economy and in particular the effects of industrial agriculture on local farmers and their communities.

One of the most sweeping points made by the Asilomar Declaration calls for a shift in the United States from industrial to sustainable agriculture. In this scenario, the US would take a leadership position in encouraging global institutions such as the Agency for International Development (USAID), the World Bank, the World Trade Organization (WTO), and the International Monetary Fund (IMF) to promote sustainable farming practices. As one of the key world food producers, the US is a logical choice for leadership in promoting sustainable farming. The spread of farmers' markets, Community Supported Agriculture (CSA) programs and Local Employment Trading System (LETS) in the US and Europe shows strong public support for local farmers and communities.

The Europeans also have had a tremendous impact in leading strong opposition to genetically altered foods. In 2004, Mendocino County, California, became the first county in the United States to ban genetically modified plants and animals. This action has sparked similar initiatives in numerous other US counties.

The Seven Challenges in the Asilomar Declaration for Sustainable Agriculture stem from efforts begun in the early 1980s by the Alliance for Sustainability, which envisions "the worldwide realization of sustainable agriculture — food systems which are ecologically sound, economically viable, socially just and humane."[20] The Alliance for Sustainability's definition of sustainable agriculture encompasses the Three Es (ecology, economy, equity) within a framework that defines the challenges of achieving sustainable agriculture.

THe Asilomar Declaration
for sustainable agriculture[21]

The present system for American agriculture cannot long endure. Our farms have succeeded in producing abundant food and fiber. But the costs and fragility of that success are becoming each day more evident.

Sustainable alternatives already prove their value. Not only are they more efficient in their use of energy, biological sources of fertility and pest management, they also enhance rural communities and encourage families to remain on the land. We commit ourselves to hastening the broad adoption of an agriculture that is ecologically sound, economically viable, fair, and humane.

A sustainable agriculture will require and support a sustainable society. Our challenge is to meet human needs without denying our descendants' birthright to the natural inheritance of this planet. We must revere the earth, sustaining and regenerating both nature and our communities. People are a part of nature, not separate from it. Sustainable agriculture is as attainable as it is necessary. Though we recognize difficulties in this transformation, we can state with confidence that in every region there are farm families profitably growing healthy food through a practical partnership with nature.

A sustainable agriculture that provides nourishing food, protects those who work the land, helps stabilize the earth's climate, and safeguards soil and water depends on our ability to meet a number of challenges. We must address those challenges with-out delay.

Seven challenges

Promote and sustain healthy rural communities.
Healthy rural communities are attractive and equitable for farmers, farm workers, and their families. The continuation of traditional values and farming wisdom depends on a stable,

multi-generational population. Absentee or corporate land ownership and the ever-increasing size of farms diminish rural life.

Expand opportunities for new and existing farmers to prosper using sustainable systems.

We must devise ways to help people get started in sustainable farming. Reliable information on sustainable agriculture needs to be readily available to farmers, extension agents, bankers, and others. Training and apprenticeship programs should be provided for entry-level farmers and established conventional farmers interested in making the transition. Tax forgiveness and other incentives should be devised to ease the financial stress of new and transitional farmers.

Inspire the public to value safe and healthy food.

The biological quality of food is known to affect the health and well-being of those who eat it. Food quality is a key factor in disease prevention. Approaches which are striving to be sustainable — such as organic farming — avoid hazardous pesticide use and maintain nutrient balance. Consumers' understanding of these facts will increase their willingness to pay prices that reflect the true costs of production.

Foster an ethic of land stewardship and humaneness in the treatment of farm animals.

Sustainable agriculture recognizes that the gifts of nature upon which it depends — soil, water, plants, animals, both wild and domestic — are to be treated with loving care and humility. The greatest calling of the farmer is to leave those gifts in better condition than when they were received. Such a responsible agriculture can only be achieved when nature is both mentor and model, and when natural systems are the standard against which success is measured. Farm animals often contribute to ecologically sound agricultural systems and they deserve humane care.

Expand knowledge access to information about sustainable agriculture.

American farmers are innovators. Given scientifically validated techniques, farmers will adopt sustainable agricultural practices.

Seeing these practices in the field will speed adoption. We need demonstration farms, farmer-to-farmer field tours, and studies of alternative farms of all sizes. University teaching, research, and extension must be redirected toward understanding the whole farm ecology and away from chemical dependence in farm management.

Reform the relationship among government, industry, and agriculture.

Government must use resources such as subsidies, grants, and loans to convert significant portions of industrial agriculture to a sustainable system. Undue rewards to concentrated interests should be replaced with fair returns to farmers who sustainably provide food and fiber.

Redefine the role of U.S. agriculture in the global community.

The present global agriculture trade is placing unnecessary pressures on the sustainability of the earth's resource base. The United States has a unique opportunity to change that situation. The people of many other countries look to us for agricultural leadership. We can honor that respect by restricting our trade in dangerous substances. We can encourage the Agency for International Development, The World Bank, and international research institutions to convert to sustainable programs. The international programs of universities can become centers of sustainability training and research.

One of the main points of the Asilomar Declaration is the need to preserve and promote the farming lifestyle and rural communities. The threat to this fundamental way of life from large corporations purchasing family farms is one of the most visible signs of the influence of corporate America on the farming industry. Since small farmers cannot compete with large agribusiness farms, the declaration states: "Undue rewards to concentrated interests should be replaced with fair returns to farmers who sustainably provide food and fiber."

The Asilomar Declaration includes sustainability education for farmers and the public. Training and apprenticeship programs would expand organic farming, thereby reducing the cost of organic produce. Educating the public about organic farming would encourage consumers to pay the "true costs" of agricultural products, since many current government subsidies conceal the actual costs of growing and transporting food.

Understanding of the true costs of food products requires a systems perspective that examines the numerous steps in preparation, production, packing, shipping and final delivery. In the case of vegetables, for example, the true costs include the farmer's cost of preparing the soil, controlling pests, irrigating and harvesting; the cost of the energy required to package the product; and the cost of the energy and air pollution involved in transporting the product to the local market, where it is kept until it is purchased.

In effect, international trade agreements and the global transportation network mask the true ecological, economic and social costs.

Developed nations such as the United States import a wide range of off-season food items, including apples from Chile and mussels from New Zealand, that are transported thousands of miles by air and then trucked nationwide to local supermarkets. These items are resource-intensive goods that also disrupt local economies by tying them to the price fluctuations of international markets. In effect, international trade agreements and the global transportation network mask the true ecological, economic and social costs.

Two innovative sustainable agriculture programs are Protected Harvest and the Code of Sustainable Winegrowing Practices. As an independent certifying organization, Protected Harvest was established in 2001 by the collaboration of the World Wildlife Fund, the Wisconsin Potato and Vegetable Growers Association and the University of Wisconsin with a mission of "advancing and certifying the use of environmentally and economically sustainable agriculture practices through the development of stringent, transparent and quantifiable standards, incentive-based eco-labeling and public education."[22]

The Protected Harvest standards pertain to specific environmental conditions of each crop and bioregion and focus on production (including pest, weed and disease management and soil and water quality); toxicity (staying below a total number of "toxicity units" per acre and prohibiting the most highly toxic pesticides); and chain of custody (auditing the crop from the field to the retail stores). Protected Harvest's certification program has been successfully implemented on 10,000 acres of Wisconsin's potatoes, with potatoes carrying the seal in supermarkets in the Midwest and on the East Coast. Protected Harvest aims to develop standards for 20 new crops in the coming years.[23]

The Code of Sustainable Winegrowing Practices (SWP) was established in 2002 by the Wine Institute and the California Association of Winegrape Growers (CAWG) to "promote environmental stewardship and social responsibility in the California wine industry."[24] As a self-assessment tool, the SWP code is detailed in a comprehensive workbook that assists vintners and growers in working with issues such as soil, water, pest and solid waste management as well as employee, neighborhood and community relationships.

In essence, the SWP code lays out a set of sustainability strategies for the wine industry that are "Environmentally Sound, Economically Feasible and Socially Equitable."[25] Presently, about 50 percent of California's wine production and 30 percent of its vineyards have been assessed using the code. Internationally, wine-growing countries including Australia, New Zealand, South Africa, Chile, Argentina, France, Germany, Italy and Peru are interested in reviewing the SWP standards for their own programs.

A new farming ethic is emerging. Emphasizing land stewardship and the humane treatment of animals, the Asilomar Declaration takes a systems approach in which the interrelationships of soil, water, plants and wild and domestic animals are considered by the farmer. The new ethic involves respect for the lessons we can learn from nature: "Such a responsible agriculture can only be achieved when nature is both mentor and model, and when natural systems are the standard against which success is measured." By adopting nature as a standard, we rely on the success of processes that have evolved over billions of years and that can give us the knowledge we need to implement sustainable farming practices.

Natural Resources at a Crossroads

The Natural Resources principles are grounded in industries that have a direct and often damaging impact on the Earth. The principles highlight the changes necessary for developing sustainable practices in the extraction industries. These industries also have had a major impact on the economic development of nations. However, we are now at a crossroads and must shift from fossil fuels to renewable energy sources and from unsustainable to sustainable practices in logging, fishing and farming.

CHAPTER 5

Sustainability and Ecological Design

What is the good of having a nice house without a decent planet to put it on?

—Henry David Thoreau

Human subtlety will never devise an invention more beautiful, more simple or more direct than does Nature, because in her inventions, nothing is lacking and nothing is superfluous.

—Leonardo da Vinci

Designing with Nature

The Sustainability and Ecological Design principles examine the interdependence of human environments and ecosystems and point to the far-reaching effects that design decisions have on the environment. The statistics for the environmental impacts of buildings are staggering. In the United States, buildings are responsible for over 65 percent of total electricity consumption, 30 percent of total greenhouse gas emissions, 136 million tons per year of construction and demolition waste (approximately 2.8 pounds per person per day) and 12 percent of potable water use. Globally, buildings use 40 percent (3 billion tons annually) of all raw materials.[1] Given the magnitude of the built environment, finding alternative building strategies that are in harmony with communities and ecosystems is imperative.

The benefits of sustainable or "green" building practices extend beyond reducing environmental impacts. Green building strategies also make wise business sense by promoting economic savings through reduced operating costs, by improving health and safety for occupants and visitors and by enhancing quality of life in local communities.

The principles of ecological design focus on the interaction of architecture, people and nature. They use environmental impacts (both positive and negative) to evaluate design and product life cycle and reinterpret the concept of waste. They explore the benefits of regenerative design, which goes beyond limiting environmental impact and strives to enhance our life-support systems. These principles also take a broad perspective that incorporates cultural, spiritual and historical traditions into the design process. Although the Sustainability and Ecological Design principles effectively integrate the environment (the First E of sustainability) into the design process, except in the Sanborn Principles economy/employment (Second E) and equity/equality (Third E) issues are not thoroughly investigated.

We will explore the general implications of the principles and then look at the significant points of each of the frameworks: William McDonough Architects' Hannover Principles, Sim Van der Ryn and Stuart Cowan's Five Principles of Ecological Design, John and Nancy Jack Todd's Principles of Ecological Design, the Sanborn Principles and the LEED (Leadership in Energy and Environmental Design) Green Building Rating System®.

The Hannover Principles, written by architect William McDonough and chemist Michael Braungart, provide a holistic perspective on the tasks and responsibilities of architects; Sim Van der Ryn and Stuart Cowan's Five Principles of Ecological Design illustrate simple ways of integrating nature into the design process; John and Nancy Jack Todd's Principles of Ecological Design bring an innovative fusion of biology and engineering to their design solutions; the Sanborn Principles mesh natural and cultural resources with the built environment; and the LEED Green Building Rating

System provides a powerful framework and standardized tool for implementing and measuring sustainability strategies in high-performance buildings.

The Hannover Principles

The framework for the Hannover Principles is based on the elements of Earth, Air, Fire, Water and Spirit. Sustainable design decisions are to be made within the context of these elements. One of the essential points of the Hannover Principles is that humans must coexist with nature. Implicit in this idea is our interdependence with the natural world, including the effects of design on the viability of ecosystems. The Hannover Principles consider "all aspects of human settlement," going beyond physical structure to encompass the interactions of people with their built environment and with nature.

It is important to understand efficient energy use and the life cycles of products. Although embodied energy — the energy required to manufacture products — is not always considered, it can play a significant role in the environmental impact of a building project. The life-cycle concept speaks to the phases and costs (both economic and ecologic) of a product from its initial design to its use and eventual disposal.

The "cradle to cradle" approach to product life cycle requires that products be reintegrated into the manufacturing process or biodegrade. Rather than designing products with limited reusability ("cradle to grave"), designers use resources and design systems that support reuse in new products and services that support the manufacturing and ecological cycles. The cradle to cradle concept, explored by business management and industrial anaylsis consultant Walter Stahel from the Product-Life Institute in Geneva[2] and by McDonough and Braungart in *Cradle to Cradle: Remaking the Way We Make Things* (2002), is redefining how we design products and systems to integrate them into a regenerative cycle.

The Hannover Principles were developed by William McDonough Architects for EXPO 2000, the World's Fair for the year 2000 in Hannover, Germany. The theme for EXPO 2000, "Humanity, Nature, and Technology," incorporated the elements of ecological design. The principles were conceived "to inform the international design community of the issues inherent in the consideration of sustainable design, rather than to provide an ecological check list for construction."[3]

The Hannover Principles[4]

1. **Insist on rights of humanity and nature to co-exist** in a healthy, supportive, diverse and sustainable condition.

2. **Recognize interdependence.** The elements of human design interact with and depend upon the natural world, with broad and diverse implications at every scale. Expand design considerations to recognizing even distant effects.

3. **Respect relationships between spirit and matter.** Consider all aspects of human settlement including community, dwelling, industry and trade in terms of existing and evolving connections between spiritual and material consciousness.

4. **Accept responsibility for the consequences of design** decisions upon human well-being, the viability of natural systems and their right to co-exist.

5. **Create safe objects of long-term value.** Do not burden future generations with requirements for maintenance or vigilant administration of potential danger due to the careless creation of products, processes or standards.

6. **Eliminate the concept of waste.** Evaluate and optimize the full life-cycle of products and processes to approach the state of natural systems, in which there is no waste.

7. **Rely on natural energy flows.** Human designs should, like the living world, derive their creative forces from perpetual solar income. Incorporate this energy efficiently and safely for responsible use.

8. **Understand the limitations of design.** No human creation lasts forever and design does not solve all problems. Those who create and plan should practice humility in the face of nature. Treat nature as a model and mentor, not as an inconvenience to be evaded or controlled.

9. **Seek constant improvement by the sharing of knowledge.** Encourage direct and open communication between colleagues, patrons, manufacturers and users to link long term sustainable considerations with ethical responsibility, and re-establish the integral relationship between natural processes and human activity.

The Hannover Principles should be seen as a living document committed to the transformation and growth in the understanding of our interdependence with nature, so that they may adapt as our knowledge of the world evolves.

The Hannover principles successfully address the interdependence of humanity and nature. This relationship manifests itself in accepting "responsibility for the consequences of design" — that is, recognizing our need to coexist with nature, eliminating waste and developing products and services aligned with this vision.

In *Cradle to Cradle*, McDonough and Braungart identify two metabolisms: biological and technical. The biological metabolism, or biosphere, refers to the cycles of nature and the technical metabolism, or technosphere, refers to the cycles of industry. For these metabolisms to remain healthy, valuable and successful, they should not mix or contaminate each other. As in nature, the concept of waste does not exist in these two cycles.[5]

Products are divided into three categories: products of consumption, products of service or durables and unmarketables. Products of consumption are those made from materials that will biodegrade and become organic nutrients in the biosphere. Products of service or durables (such as cars, televisions, carpets, computers and refrigerators) are licensed rather than sold. When such a product has outlived its use, it is returned to the manufacturer for reintegration into the manufacturing cycle as a "technical nutrient" or industrial "food" for the technosphere. Finally, the unmarketables are toxic and hazardous products, such as nuclear waste and polyvinyl chloride (PVC), which should be securely stored until we have developed the technology to detoxify or safely dispose of them.[6]

The Hannover Principles' "long-term value" emphasizes the challenge and responsibility to design structures, products and standards that broaden rather than restrict the possibilities for future generations. The limitations of design and of ourselves should lead us to "practice humility in the face of nature" and to learn about natural processes through observation and practice.

Although tailored for EXPO 2000, the Hannover Principles provide an innovative framework for sustainable design concepts with broad applications. The sense of humility and the sharing of knowledge illustrate the need for cooperation and partnership to seek lasting solutions to design problems. This realistic appraisal provides a refreshing look at the design industry. As William McDonough Architects state: "The Hannover EXPO is based on ideas of restraint, awareness, and concern for solving the world's problems, not hiding them behind a wall of promising machines."[7]

The Five Principles of Ecological Design

Sim Van der Ryn and Stuart Cowan's Five Principles of Ecological Design highlight the importance of understanding the local setting and designing structures that complement natural processes. One of their essential points deals with the sense of place. Knowledge and understanding of a proposed site plays a critical role in shaping the design process. When we become familiar with the nuances of a place, solutions reveal themselves.

These principles reiterate the importance of integrating design with nature to regenerate rather than deplete the ecosystem. Van der Ryn and Cowan challenge us to make "natural cycles and processes visible" by working with sunlight, water, temperature fluctuations and seasonal variations in our design structures. The more seamlessly these factors are integrated into the design, the less our activities will detract from the health of nature. Our awareness of the short- and long-term impacts of design on nature will help us determine ecologically sound design possibilities.

The Five Principles of Ecological Design stem from Sim Van der Ryn and Stuart Cowan's groundbreaking book *Ecological Design* (1995), which explores the integration of sustainability concepts and ecological design. The Five Principles clearly articulate the interdependence of design, function and nature. The principles are being implemented in the work of the Ecological Design Institute (EDI) and Sim Van der Ryn Architects.

The five principles of ecological design[8]

1. **Solutions Grow from Place.** Ecological design begins with the intimate knowledge of a particular place. Therefore, it is small scale and direct, responsive to both local conditions and local people. If we are sensitive to the nuances of place, we can inhabit without destroying.

2. **Ecological Accounting Informs Design.** Trace the environmental impacts of existing or proposed designs. Use this information to determine the most ecologically sound design possibility.

3. **Design with Nature.** By working with living processes, we respect the needs of all species while meeting our own. Engaging in processes that regenerate rather than deplete, we become more alive.

4. **Everyone is a Designer.** Listen to every voice in the design process. No one is participant only or designer only. Everyone is a participant-designer. Honor the special knowledge that each person brings. As people work together to heal their places, they also heal themselves.

5. **Make Nature Visible.** Denatured environments ignore our need and potential for learning. Making natural cycles and processes visible brings the designed environment back to life. Effective design helps inform us of our place within nature.

"Listen to every voice in the design process" emphasizes the value of cooperation from a variety of individuals with multidisciplinary perspectives. Linking nature's well-being with our own, the principles point out: "As people work together to heal their places, they also heal themselves." The focus on oneself, one's place and the natural processes brings together the key concepts in sustainable ecological design.

The Todds' Principles of Ecological Design

The search for lasting design solutions from a biological perspective is exemplified in the work of John and Nancy Jack Todd. The Todds' principles provide a biological framework that places nature at the center of the design process. As the "matrix for all design," the natural world is designated as the reservoir for ecological designers. Nature is both the teacher and the inspiration for design. The Todds emphasize that design must follow "the laws of life" — in other words, design must be in alignment with nature's fundamental laws and processes. The concept of "biological equity," which is covered widely by the principles in the Sustainability and the Biosphere chapter, focuses on the impact of design decisions on other species. The built environment, which arises from design decisions, often has catastrophic impacts on the environment.

John and Nancy Jack Todd's Principles of Ecological Design stem from their book *From Eco-cities to Living Machines* (1994). The Todds co-founded the New Alchemy Institute and later Ocean Arks International and Living Technologies. Their work in ecological design incorporates aspects of energy, architecture, food production and waste management. Their living machines use microorganisms and plants to purify and reclaim water.

Principles of ecological design[9]

1. The living world is the matrix for all design.
2. Design should follow, not oppose, the laws of life.
3. Biological equity must determine design.
4. Design must reflect bioregionality.
5. Projects should be based on renewable energy sources.
6. Design should be sustainable through the integration of living systems.
7. Design should be coevolutionary with the natural world.
8. Building and design should help heal the planet.
9. Design should follow a sacred ecology.

In stating that design must "reflect bioregionality" and be "coevolutionary with the natural world," the Todds touch on the significance of the local ecosystem in the design process. The bioregion in many respects determines the local characteristics that, if carefully studied and observed, will point to an efficient design. The coevolution of design and nature illustrates the importance of creating a synergistic alliance between the designed environment and nature. In order to accommodate unforeseen changes, as nature evolves so must the built environment.

The Todds' principles have similarities to the Hannover Principles and the Five Principles of Ecological Design. As do Hannover's "recognize interdependence" and Van der Ryn and Cowan's "design with nature" principles, the Todds repeatedly emphasize how nature provides the underlying structure as the "matrix" and the "laws of life" for the design process. The connections between design and the natural world provide the biological basis of the Todds' Principles of Ecological Design. With a biological lexicon that includes the concepts of bioregions and coevolution, designers can strive to devise solutions that enhance rather than detract from the biological diversity of the natural world.

The Sanborn Principles

The Sanborn Principles apply the design values discussed by the Todds and by Van der Ryn and Cowan to the practical needs of a community. The Sanborn Principles successfully integrate social and ecological needs. Like Van der Ryn and Cowan's "design with nature" principle and the Todds' assertion that design must follow the "laws of life," the Sanborn Principles make a case for a close examination of the site and natural processes in devising design solutions. The Hannover Principles' reference to respecting the "relationships between spirit and matter" is reiterated by the Sanborn Principles' support for culturally creative and aesthetically pleasing structures.

The Sanborn Principles were developed at the Sanborn Conference, held near Colorado Springs, Colorado, in 1994. Energy consultant Barbara Harwood, numerous experts such as Amory Lovins, Paul MacCready and others in energy efficiency, renewable energy, single- and multi-family housing, anthropology, sociology, water conservation and transportation gathered there to envision crosscultural guidelines for a sustainable future. The principles provide a comprehensive approach to ecological design that considers building structure, its impact on the environment and the social, economic and esthetic implications. The principles since have been disseminated to many countries, including Canada, South Africa, Italy and Israel.

The Sanborn principles[10]

1. **Ecologically Responsive:** The Design of human habitat shall recognize that all resources are limited, and will respond to the patterns of natural ecology. Land plans and building designs will include only those with the least disruptive impact upon the natural ecology of the earth. Density must be most intense near neighborhood centers where facilities are most accessible.

2. **Healthy, Sensible Buildings:** The design of human habitat must create a living environment that will be healthy

for all its occupants. Buildings should be of appropriate human scale in a non-sterile, aesthetically pleasing environment. Building design must respond to toxicity of materials, care with EMF, lighting efficiency and quality, comfort requirements and resource efficiency. Buildings should be organic, integrate art, natural materials, sunlight, green plants, energy efficiency, low noise levels and water. They should not cost more than current conventional buildings. Features of the buildings and their surroundings should include:

a. No waste that cannot be assimilated.

b. Thermal responsiveness.

c. Reflective or actively productive roofing or parking cover surfaces.

d. Junglified or planted with native vegetation, both exterior and interior.

e. Access by foot to primary services.

f. Natural corridors near residences for wildlife.

g. Individual and/or community gardens.

h. Local agriculture for local consumption.

3. **Socially Just:** Habitats shall be equally accessible across economic classes.

4. **Culturally Creative:** Habitats will allow ethnic groups to maintain individual cultural identities and neighborhoods while integrating into the larger community. All population groups shall have access to art, theater and music.

5. **Beautiful:** Beauty in a habitat environment is necessary for the soul development of human beings. It is yeast for the ferment of individual creativity. Intimacy with the beauty and numinous mystery of nature must be available to enliven our sense of the sacred.

6. **Physically and Economically Accessible:** All sites within the habitat shall be accessible and rich in resources to those living within walkable (or wheelchair-able) distance. Accessible characteristics shall include:

   a. Radical traffic calming.

   b. Clean, accessible, economical mass transit.

   c. Bicycle paths.

   d. Small neighborhood service businesses; i.e. bakeries, tailors, groceries, fish and meat markets, delis, coffee bars, etc.

   e. Places to go where chances of accidental meetings are high; i.e. neighborhood parks, playgrounds, cafes, sports centers, community centers, etc.

7. **Evolutionary:** Habitats' design shall include continuous re-evaluation of premises and values, shall be demographically responsive and flexible to change over time to support future user needs. Initial designs should reflect our society's heterogeneity and have a feedback system. They shall be:

   a. Villagified

   b. Multigenerational

   c. Non-exclusionary

One of the key features of the Sanborn Principles is the concept of health for building occupants and the environment. A building should be "healthy for all its occupants ... of appropriate human scale ... and aesthetically pleasing ...." In addition, building design must be responsive to toxic materials, electromagnetic fields (EMF), lighting, comfort and resource efficiency.

These parameters focus on the relationship between people's needs and activities and a building's capacity for accommodating them. Although comfort and esthetics are difficult to quantify, building occupants know when a building is a comfortable and pleasant place to live and work.

To preserve the health of the ecosystem, the Sanborn Principles focus on having minimal impact on the "patterns of natural ecology." This concept, similar to those of permaculture (discussed in Sustainability and the Biosphere), advocates observing and learning from nature.

The Sanborn Principles also touch on social equity in building construction. "Habitats shall be equally accessible across economic classes" implies a commitment to providing affordable housing for everyone. The principles also promote accessible mass transit, traffic calming and the creation of places that bring people from the neighborhood together. In addition, the principles aim to maintain the character and cultural identity of ethnic groups within a neighborhood by creating environments that support human interactions.

The notion of beauty, mentioned by these principles, is difficult to define, yet speaks to the quality of life for individual community members, an important aspect of sustainability. The beauty of buildings is enhanced when they are well integrated with the landscape and when their function is seamlessly meshed with their esthetic value.

In calling for a "continuous re-evaluation of premises and values," the Sanborn Principles emphasize the evolution of buildings. By advocating flexibility in building design, the principles support building techniques and structures that can easily be modified as new needs arise. Buildings become thriving structures able to change over time.

US and World Green Building Councils: The LEEDing Edge

One of the most encouraging developments within the Sustainability Revolution is the rise of the US Green Building Council with its international counterpart, the World Green Building Council, and the LEED (Leadership in Energy and Environmental Design) Green Building Rating System.[11]

Established in 1993, the US Green Building Council aims to "promote buildings that are environmentally responsible, profitable and healthy places to live and work."[12] Through the LEED products and resources, GreenBuild, the Annual International Green Building Conference and Expo, and the current 157 LEED-Certified projects and over 1,700 LEED-Registered projects in all 50 states and 13 countries, the US and World Green Building Councils are spearheading a transformation in the building industry.[13] In California, for example, in December 2004 Governor Arnold Schwarzenegger signed a landmark Green Buildings Executive Order setting a goal for state buildings to be 20 percent more energy efficient by 2015 and mandating "designing, constructing and operating all new and renovated state-owned facilities paid for with state funds as 'LEED Silver' or higher certified buildings."[14]

LEED is a rating system for designing, constructing and operating buildings. The system provides a useful standard to define the "green" aspects of buildings by evaluating areas such as: Sustainable Sites, Water Efficiency, Energy and Atmosphere, Materials and Resources, Indoor Environmental Quality and Innovation and Design Process. These categories are assigned points that challenge owners and builders to strive for Certified, Silver, Gold and Platinum certification levels.

With a diverse membership of over 5,000 organizations including manufacturers, architects, builders, nonprofits, utilities, schools and state, local and federal governments, the US Green Building Council has a powerful voice that is reverberating in the international arena. Already Brazil, Canada, China, Guatemala, India, Italy, Japan, Mexico and Netherlands Antilles have LEED-Registered projects, demonstrating that the standard can adapt to different cultures and bioregions.[15]

Though not perfect, LEED provides a powerful tool for industry professionals and owners to use in implementing sustainable strategies in their building projects. The LEED process involves third-party assessments and evaluation by technical and scientific committees to ensure unbiased conclusions and avoid "green washing" (giving the false impression of being "green"). LEED products are balloted by US Green Building Council members and subsequently implemented in the marketplace.

Designed to continually evolve as knowledge in the industry increases, the LEED system challenges its adopters to use a longer time-horizon when evaluating the costs and benefits of "green" projects. As the LEED programs continue to expand to include commercial interiors, core and shell construction, existing buildings, neighborhood developments and the residential sector, their impact undoubtedly will continue to shape the building industry and educate the public about the significance of building "green."

An Interdependent Perspective

The principles of Sustainability and Ecological Design — Hannover Principles, The Five Principles of Ecological Design, Todds' Principles, Sanborn Principles and LEED — recognize the interdependence of design and nature. The theme of nature as teacher and model, discussed later in Sustainability and the Biosphere, also is touched upon here. Buildings are integrated into their space and ideally mesh with the patterns and cycles of the natural world without detracting from or overpowering their setting.

McDonough and Braungart challenge us to reexamine eco-efficiency and instead consider eco-effectiveness in ecological design. Whereas eco-efficiency emphasizes reductions in resource consumption, energy use, emissions and waste, eco-effectiveness promotes optimal design strategies that support both human and ecological systems:

> Our concept of eco-effectiveness means working on the right things — on the right products and services and systems — instead of making the wrong things less bad .... The key is not to make human industries and systems smaller, as efficiency advocates propound, but to design them to get bigger and better in a way that replenishes, restores and nourishes the rest of the world.[16]

As McDonough and Braungart point out, the regenerative design approach may one day lead to buildings that, like trees, produce more energy than they consume and purify their waste water; factories whose "waste" is drinking water; products that when they are no longer needed can be composted in our backyards and serve as nutrients for plants and animals or be returned to the industrial cycle — in essence, a world of abundance rather than limits, pollution and waste.[17]

The Sustainability and Ecological Design principles also include cultural and spiritual values. Ecological design thus provides a thread that joins our cultural heritage with our present and future interaction with the environment and opens prospects for regeneration.

CHAPTER 6

Sustainability and the Biosphere

Look deep into nature, and then you will understand every-thing better.

—Albert Einstein

Nature does nothing uselessly.

—Aristotle

Our Role in the Biosphere

THE RELATIONSHIP BETWEEN HUMANS AND NATURE lies at the center of sustainability. Since our impact on the natural world is powerful, widespread and often detrimental, new perspectives are arising regarding our place in nature. What is the role of nature as a model and teacher? How can we live in harmony with the natural world and create a vibrant and healthy economy that supports all life on the planet?

The Sustainability and the Biosphere principles address these and other questions that underlie the emerging environmental ethic. As with the ecological design principles, the biosphere principles focus mainly on ecological concerns (the First E) and only superficially address economic and equity (Second and Third E) issues. While each of the selected groups in Sustainability and the Biosphere provides guidelines for our interactions with nature, the critical links between employment and equity issues and ecological issues remain vague and inconclusive. This uneven treatment of sustainability makes it particularly challenging to ground these principles in everyday life.

The concept of nature as a valuable teacher that can guide human actions permeates this section. Many of the principles point to the quite recent (geologically speaking) appearance of humans on Earth and the 3.8 billion years of existence and experience of other life forms. The principles emphasize that we are but one strand in a complex web of life and have much to learn from other species. Moreover, since humans and all other species depend on the ecosystems in the biosphere for survival we must be especially aware of human impact and responsibility.

In our analysis of Sustainability and the Biosphere, we will explore the general implications of each set of principles and then look at the significant points of each of the specific groups: Deep Ecology's Basic Principles, the Charter of Rights and Responsibilities for the Environment, the Biomimicry Principles and the Mollisonian Permaculture Principles.

Deep Ecology's Basic Principles are philosophical and action-oriented; the Charter of Rights and Responsibilities for the Environment is policy-based; the Biomimicry Principles look at nature as a beneficial model for business and industry; and the Mollisonian Permaculture Principles take a systems approach to our relationship with the natural world.

Deep Ecology's Basic Principles

One of the most powerful themes in the deep ecology principles is the intrinsic value of non-human life. Appreciation for non-human species counters the Western development model, which seeks to exploit nature to accommodate human needs. For deep ecologists, the right of other species to exist is independent of human activities.

The deep ecology principles stem from the work of Norwegian philosopher and ecologist Arne Naess. The cornerstones of his deep ecology perspective include self-realization and biocentric equality.[1] Self-realization is the concept of being connected to other life forces. Biocentric equality means that all species have the intrinsic right to exist. Thus, deep ecology asks us to reexamine our role in the web of life. The following principles of deep ecology were developed by Arne Naess and George Sessions:

Deep ecology's basic principles[2]

1. The well-being and flourishing of human and nonhuman Life on Earth have a value in themselves (synonyms: intrinsic value, inherent value). These values are independent of the usefulness of the nonhuman world for human purposes.

2. Richness and diversity of life forms contribute to the realization of these values and are also values in themselves.

3. Humans have no right to reduce this richness and diversity except to satisfy vital needs.

4. The flourishing of human life and cultures is compatible with a substantial decrease of the human population. The flourishing of nonhuman life requires such a decrease.

5. Present human interference with the nonhuman world is excessive, and the situation is rapidly worsening.

6. Policies must therefore be changed. These policies affect the basic economic, technological, and ideological structures. The resulting state of affairs will be deeply different from the present.

7. The ideological change is mainly that of appreciating *life quality* (dwelling in situations of inherent value) rather than adhering to an increasingly higher standard of living. There will be a profound awareness of the difference between big and great.

8. Those who subscribe to the foregoing points have an obligation directly or indirectly to try to implement the necessary changes.

Naess and Sessions point to the diversity of life as an essential component of the deep ecology framework. They believe that humans should "reduce" this diversity only to "satisfy vital needs." While what constitutes a vital need is not addressed by the authors, this ambiguity leaves room for the evolution of an ethic revolving around the question of "how much is enough?"

The deep ecology philosophy also stresses the significance of "life quality," defined as "dwelling in situations of inherent value," rather than "an increasingly higher standard of living." Again, as with "vital need," "inherent value" is undefined. It involves a subtle yet profound distinction between the richness of values that support life and the desire for increased consumption — better, not bigger, or "the difference between big and great." The deep ecology principles also point out the importance of reducing human population to permit non-human life to flourish, and put forth a call for action to those who support the principles.

Charter of Rights and Responsibilities for the Environment

Deep ecology's concern for all species is extended by the principles from the Charter of Rights and Responsibilities for the Environment. The charter highlights our interdependence with the natural world. Nature is defined a community to which humans belong rather than a "commodity" for our exploitation. We have a stewardship role in protecting the essential aspects of ecosystems such as air, water and soil.

The Charter of Rights and Responsibilities for the Environment stems from the Women and Sustainable Development: Canadian Perspectives Conference held in Vancouver, Canada, in 1994. The principles were developed by Ann Dale, then at the Sustainable

Development Research Institute, who declared that "if decisions are not made and acted upon now about how to live more sustainably ... a threshold of irreversibility will be reached, and options for future generations foreclosed."[3] She proposed a legal approach based on the charter's principles that would be a powerful agent for change.

Charter of rights and responsibilities for the environment

- The biosphere is a community to which we belong rather than a commodity belonging to us.
- All species have inherent value in the biosphere.
- Human beings have stewardship for the quality of water, air and soil of the biosphere.
- The entropic throughput of natural resources should reflect their real costs as a factor in production and consumption.
- The health and well-being of humans and all other species is inseparable from the health and well-being of the biosphere.
- Development must be in harmony with the environment.
- Any production that is not sustainable cannot be counted as capital.
- Optimal allocation of human and natural resources must be in harmony with optimal scale, recognizing the finite limits of the biosphere.
- Human activity must not be conducted at the irreversible expense of other species and ecosystems.
- Diversity is integral to a sustainable society.
- Sustainable development maintains or enhances the integrity of natural resource capital, thereby contributing to the increased well-being of all species.

- The present generation has an obligation to future generations.
- The health of one nation ultimately affects the health of all nations.

The charter emphasizes the importance of taking into account the "real costs" of production and consumption. For example, the real cost of gasoline production, which is not reflected in the price at the gas station, includes the environmental destruction caused by extracting the petroleum; the military expenditures for securing oil fields, pipelines and shipping; the pollution and toxins released during refining; and the release of carbon dioxide from automobiles, which affects acid rain and global warming. The ripple effect of real costs is particularly relevant to sustainability issues confronting communities and commercial interests.

The charter also emphasizes the importance of observing the limits of the biosphere. These limits require optimizing human activities by aligning our actions with the needs and rights of other species. The sense of responsibility for ecosystems extends to an obligation of the present generation to future generations. This long-term perspective underscores a deep commitment to core values that support a responsible outlook to the future.

Biomimicry Principles

In her book, *Biomimicry* (1997), Janine Benyus describes how nature serves as a viable model, as a measure and as a mentor worthy of imitation by humans. "Biomimicry" comes from the Greek *bios* (life) and *mimesis* (imitation). As a model, nature provides insights in our quest for design solutions. For example, navigation in bats is the basis for radar technology, and architectural designs are derived from the structure of lily pads and bamboo shoots. As a measure or ecological standard, nature with its 3.8 billion years of evolution acts as a guide for humans. As a mentor, nature teaches humans to treat ecosystems not as a commodity but as a source of knowledge and inspiration.

The Biomimicry Principles focus exclusively on nature's attributes, implying that humans have much to learn from the natural world's evolutionary experience. Benyus portrays the significance of natural optimization of resources by stating that nature "uses only the energy it needs," "recycles everything," and "curbs excesses from within." Nature's optimization stands in sharp contrast to the inefficient use of nonrenewable energy sources, the tremendous waste in manufacturing and disposal habits and the excessive consumption in the industrialized nations.

Biomimicry principles [5]

- Nature runs on sunlight.
- Nature uses only the energy it needs.
- Nature fits form to function.
- Nature recycles everything.
- Nature rewards cooperation.
- Nature banks on diversity.
- Nature demands local expertise.
- Nature curbs excesses from within.
- Nature taps the power of limits.

From an ecosystem perspective, the Biomimicry Principles point out the significance of cooperation and diversity, the antithesis of the competitive nature of our economic system and our reliance on monocultures. Benyus makes the interesting observation that nature "taps the power of limits." This principle recognizes how species maximize the benefits of the constraints of ecosystems in, for example, temperature range, seasonal variations and soil fertility. Within these boundaries, nature flourishes. In contrast, she states that "humans regard limits as a universal dare, something to be overcome so we can continue our expansion."[5] The numerous examples of biomimicry projects in agriculture, health, materials and energy production and computers indicate the potential of her inspiring principles.

Permaculture Principles

David Holmgren and Bill Mollison co-created the concepts of permaculture in the 1970s. Mollison defines permaculture (derived from "permanent agriculture" and "permanent culture") as:

> the conscious design and maintenance of agriculturally productive ecosystems which have the diversity, stability, and resilience of natural ecosystems. It is the harmonious integration of landscape and people providing their food, energy, shelter, and other material and non-material needs in a sustainable way. Without permanent agriculture there is no possibility of a stable social order.[6]

Permaculture provides a systems approach for implementing architectural, energy, agricultural and community designs, among others. Like biomimicry, which recognizes the value of learning from nature, permaculture articulates a comprehensive design strategy based on knowledge gained through observing the patterns in nature. Patterning involves grasping the significance of these patterns by looking at characteristics such as shapes, branching, pulsing, waves, matrices, form and substance. The patterns furnish a template for designing systems that are interdependent and support each other in beneficial ways.[7]

Permaculture expands the scope of biomimicry by exploring ways of integrating sustainability concepts into economic and social endeavors from implementing alternative political systems, including bioregional organization, to new property arrangements, finance systems such as the Permaculture Credit Union[8] and right livelihood.

Mollisonian permaculture principles [9]

1. Work with nature, rather than against the natural elements, forces, pressures, processes, agencies, and evolutions, so that we assist rather than impede natural developments.

2. The problem is the solution; everything works both ways. It is only how we see things that makes them advantageous or not (if the wind blows cold, let us use both its strength and its coolness to advantage). A corollary of this principle is that everything is a positive resource; it is just up to us to work out how we may use it as such.

3. Make the least change for the greatest possible effect.

4. The yield of a system is theoretically unlimited. The only limit on the number of uses of a resource possible within a system is in the limit of the information and the imagination of the designer.

5. Everything gardens, or has an effect on its environment.

The Mollisonian Permaculture Principles stress the importance of efficiency by advising us to work with nature, find the positive resource in an apparently negative situation and make "the least change for the greatest possible effect." Efficiency is rooted in allowing nature to lead in our design solutions.

The principles emphasize the critical role of information and imagination. While information undoubtedly is essential for decision making, the wise interpretation of information (not mentioned) is paramount in achieving lasting solutions. Imagination brings forth creativity in searching for ways to work with nature. Permaculture's systems approach is a powerful tool for creating a comprehensive perspective. Its focus on the relationships among species, natural forces and human habitation reveals the subtle nuances that characterize viable life-support systems.

Another set of principles that takes into account human interaction with the biosphere is the National Park Service's Guiding Principles of Sustainable Design. These principles establish a framework for designing and implementing sustainable practices through interpretive programs, natural and cultural resources and park facilities maintenance and operations. The National Ski Areas Association's Environmental Charter, Sustainable Slopes, explores the environmental impact of the ski industry and presents guidelines that include ways of reducing energy and water consumption and protecting habitats.[10]

A Biocentric Perspective

The four groups of principles in Sustainability and the Biosphere — Deep Ecology, the Charter of Rights and Responsibilities for the Environment, Biomimicry and Permaculture — present a biocentric approach to sustainability. Nature is at the center and humans depend on it for knowledge, inspiration and survival. Recurring themes in the Sustainability and the Biosphere principles include the value of non-human species, interdependence and cooperation and planning for the well-being of future generations. Many of these principles stress the need for practical approaches to respecting and working within nature's limits.

The biocentric viewpoint focuses on the importance of nature in maintaining Earth's basic life-support systems. However, it pays less attention to the economic and equity (Second and Third E) aspects of sustainability. The inevitable interdependence of ecological issues with economic and equity issues provides a critical perspective for understanding the complexity of sustainability.

CHAPTER 7

Future Pathways

*I've grown impatient with the kind of debate we used to have
about whether the optimists or the pessimists are right.
Neither are right. There is too much bad news to justify com-
placency. There is too much good news to justify despair.*
— Donella Meadows

The best way to predict the future is to invent it.
— Alan Kay

Principles: Scopes, Sectors and Types

THE SUSTAINABILITY PRINCIPLES we have investigated in Community, Commerce, Natural Resources, Ecological Design and the Biosphere vary in scope, social sector and type. The principles range in scope from local to regional, national and international. They originate from government, business and industry, civil society or a coalition of stakeholders. While some principles focus strictly on values, others include a defined methodology or standard for implementation and evaluation. (See Figure 1 for details.) We also have examined environmental management tools such as ISO 14000, the Global Reporting Initiative (GRI) and the Ecological Footprint, which stand alone and provide useful metrics for implementing the sustainability principles.

Figure 1: Comparison of Sustainability Principles

NOTE: Principles are listed according to year established. In many instances, earlier drafts of principles and concepts were in circulation. Sector categories are adapted from the International Institute for Sustainable Development (IISD) website.

NAME	YEAR Established	SCOPE				SECTOR				TYPE	
		Local	Regional	National	International	Government	Business/Industry	Civil Society	Multi-stake	Values	Metrics/Standards
Permaculture Principles	1978				✓			✓	✓	✓	
Deep Ecology's Basic Principles	1984				✓			✓	✓	✓	
Holistic Management® Model	1984				✓			✓	✓	✓	
Life Cycle Assessment (LCA)	1984				✓		✓		✓	✓	✓
CERES Principles	1989			✓				✓	✓	✓	
Cradle to Cradle	1989				✓		✓		✓	✓	
Netherlands National Environmental Policy Plan (NEPP)	1989			✓		✓			✓	✓	✓
The Natural Step	1989				✓			✓	✓	✓	
Asilomar Declaration for Sustainable Agriculture	1990			✓				✓	✓	✓	
Ecological Footprint	1990				✓			✓	✓	✓	✓
International Council of Local Environment Initiatives (ICLEI)	1990				✓	✓			✓	✓	✓
International Chamber of Commerce (ICC) Business Charter	1991				✓		✓		✓	✓	
Ontario Round Table on Environment and Economy (ORTEE) Model Principles	1992	✓				✓			✓	✓	

NAME	YEAR Established	SCOPE				SECTOR				TYPE	
		Local	Regional	National	International	Government	Business / Industry	Civil Society	Multi-stake	Values	Metrics/ Standards
The Precautionary Principle	1992				✓	✓	✓		✓	✓	
Forest Stewardship Council (FSC) Principles & Criteria of Forest Stewardship	1993				✓						✓
Charter of Rights and Responsibilities for the Environment	1994			✓				✓	✓	✓	
National Park Service's Guiding Principles	1994			✓		✓				✓	
The Sanborn Principles	1994				✓		✓		✓	✓	
The Todds' Principles of Ecological Design	1994				✓			✓		✓	
Five Principles of Ecological Design	1995				✓		✓	✓		✓	
American Petroleum Institute (API) Environmental, Health & Safety Principles	1996			✓			✓			✓	
International Standards Organization (ISO) 14000	1996				✓		✓		✓		✓
The Bellagio Principles for Assessment	1996				✓			✓	✓	✓	
Biomimicry Principles	1997				✓			✓	✓	✓	
Global Reporting Initiative (GRI)	1997				✓	✓			✓		✓
Marine Stewardship Council (MSC) Principles & Criteria for Sustainable Fishing	1997				✓					✓	

NAME	YEAR Established	SCOPE				SECTOR				TYPE	
		Local	Regional	National	International	Government	Business/Industry	Civil Society	Multi-stake	Values	Metrics/Standards
LEED Green Building Rating System®	1998				✓				✓	✓	✓
Principles of Sustainable Development for Minnesota	1998		✓			✓			✓	✓	
Global Sullivan Principles of Social Responsibility	1999				✓			✓	✓	✓	
The Houston Principles	1999			✓				✓	✓	✓	
Natural Capitalism Principles	1999				✓			✓	✓	✓	
The Earth Charter	2000				✓	✓			✓	✓	
Environmental Charter (National Ski Areas Association)	2000			✓			✓			✓	
The Hannover Principles	2000				✓		✓		✓	✓	
United Nations Global Compact	2000				✓	✓			✓	✓	
Protected Harvest Standards	2001			✓				✓	✓	✓	✓
The Code of Sustainable Winegrowing Practices (SWP)	2002				✓		✓	✓	✓	✓	✓
Sustainable Project Appraisal Routine (SPeAR®)	2002				✓		✓		✓	✓	✓
The Equator Principles	2003				✓	✓	✓	✓	✓	✓	

Although principles such as those of the Earth Charter and the American Petroleum Institute (API) point toward a pathway to sustainable development, they lack a well-defined methodology for implementation. The Natural Step and the CERES Principles also provide an open-ended framework without a specific methodology. Fortunately, environmental management tools such as ISO 14000, Life Cycle Assessment (LCA) and the Global Reporting Initiative (GRI) can be utilized with these business frameworks for implementation strategies and performance evaluation.

Certain principles are taking their industries by storm and attracting a wide range of adopters in just a few years. Why, for example, are principles of the Forest Stewardship Council (FSC), Leadership in Energy and Environmental Design (LEED) and the Code of Sustainable Winegrowing Practices (SWP) rapidly gaining such wide-ranging acceptance and becoming industry standards? Perhaps the answer is that these frameworks couple principles with criteria and methodologies that, though not prescriptive, are rigorous, well-defined and easily implemented. The FSC principles include criteria, indicators and verifiers that provide a comprehensive approach to evaluating concerns such as social equity and chain of custody. Similarly, LEED provides a flexible yet well-defined rating system for achieving its various certification levels. LEED and The Natural Step also evaluate the systems approach for designing and operating high-performance buildings and businesses. The Code of Sustainable Winegrowing Practices includes a comprehensive workbook for implementing, tracking and assessing sustainable practices.

Another reason for the rapid adoption of these principles worldwide may be that their comprehensive theoretical and practical approach is easily transferred to organizations in other cultures. In addition, perhaps their respective industries are well-positioned for an alternative business model promoting sustainable strategies that yield economic growth and increase cooperation.

Seven Common Themes

Along with the differences, there are remarkable similarities in the key values expressed by the organizations responsible for the sustainability principles. Although the Three Es (ecology, economy, equity) are emphasized to a greater or lesser extent in each set of principles, there are seven common themes. While the emphasis on these themes varies among the frameworks we have discussed, together the themes paint a comprehensive portrait of the Sustainability Revolution today. The seven themes are:

1. Stewardship

2. Respect for limits

3. Interdependence

4. Economic restructuring

5. Fair distribution

6. Intergenerational perspective

7. Nature as a model and teacher

1. **Stewardship** emphasizes the importance of establishing an ecological ethic for managing and preserving the biological integrity of ecosystems. This ethic includes safeguarding the health of resources such as water, air, soil and species biodiversity. It also incorporates promoting the use of natural building materials and renewable energy sources such as wind and solar power.

2. **Respect for limits** calls for living within nature's means by preventing waste, pollution and unsustainable resource depletion. Inherent in this theme is the protection of biodiversity, the fabric of life threatened by overconsumption in developed nations. The "limits" represent the threshold of living systems and violating these limits has devastating effects ranging from species extinction to global warming.

3. **Interdependence** covers not only the ecological relationships between species and nature but also economic and cultural ties at the local, regional and international levels. We depend on

ecological, economic and social systems that are inextricably linked to one another. Our elaborate transportation and communications systems, food and energy production, financial transactions and manufacturing capabilities rely on a vast interconnected and interdependent network. At the foundation of this network lie nature's interdependent systems providing such resources as air, water and soils, which support our survival.

4. **Economic restructuring** appears in many principles as a need for expanding employment opportunities while safeguarding ecosystems. Fostering sustainable practices depends on a new economic model based on cooperation and optimal efficiency rather than competition and waste. These new economic practices also call for government and commercial ventures to support the needs of local communities.

5. **Fair distribution** speaks to the importance of social justice and equity in areas such as employment, education and healthcare. A fair and equitable distribution of resources involves a shift in social values applied through government policies such as tax changes and through socially responsible corporate practices that address issues faced by low-income communities. Fair distribution involves creating innovative approaches for dealing with the shortcomings of the current economic model.

6. **Intergenerational perspective** emphasizes the need for a long-term rather than a short-term view to guide the critical choices facing society. By thinking about the impact of our actions on subsequent generations as far out as 150 to 500 years, we learn to prioritize our decisions. The intergenerational view clarifies the significance of society's decisions by placing them in the context of our children's, grandchildren's and great-grandchildren's lives.

7. **Nature as a model and teacher** acknowledges the 3.5 billion years of evolution of living systems and nature's significance as a reservoir of "expertise." As relative newcomers to the world's stage, humans can greatly benefit from nature's lessons. In the field of ecological design, this view of nature calls for creating

designs in accordance with the needs and cycles of the landscape. This model of nature includes respecting the rights of all non-human species.

Hopeful Signs

These common themes can be seen in some bold initiatives that demonstrate the practical implementation of the sustainability principles. Although many of the creative solutions to ecological, economic and social problems are overlooked by the mainstream press, success stories abound. Many of these inspirational stories are highlighted in the alternative press as well as on the Internet.

> ▼
>
> **Although many of the creative solutions to ecological, economic and social problems are overlooked by the mainstream press, success stories abound.**
>
> ▲

Initiatives in Gaviotas, Colombia; Curitiba, Brazil; and Kerala, India, stand out as beacons of hope.[1] In each of these areas, individuals have united to envision alternative models for solving many of the problems afflicting population centers. Gaviotas represents a vision for a village setting; Curitiba's success points to a viable future for metropolitan cities; and Kerala represents the successful integration of sustainability practices at a regional level.

In Gaviotas, an experiment to develop appropriate technologies has become a model sustainable community in the seemingly inhospitable savanna of eastern Colombia. Founder Paolo Lugari and his colleagues have succeeded in making Gaviotas self-sufficient by generating power with turbine engines powered by Caribbean pine trees, and meeting nearly all of the community's agricultural needs. The Gaviotans also have devised ingenious technologies including water pumps powered by children's seesaws, solar panels that work during the rainy season and ways of growing food without soil.

The village's economic base relies in part on harvesting natural pine resin, which is sold for use in manufacturing paint and cosmetic products. Gaviotans are using an enzyme and mycorrhiza fungus to produce twice as much resin as that produced from other resin-tapping forests.[2] The pines, planted by the Gaviotans, also have helped restore the ecosystem's native rainforest. By implementing sustainable development strategies and establishing a thriving community in one of the world's most unforgiving regions, the founders of Gaviotas have proven that such efforts can succeed elsewhere.

The city of Curitiba, Brazil, has one of the world's most successful urban planning programs. With municipal government funds, visionary planner Jaime Lerner and his staff have made buses more affordable and faster than cars for traveling in a city of 1.6 million residents — carrying over 900,000 passengers a day.[3] In addition, Curitiba has established a 16-square-mile "industrial city" near the central business district that has attracted a variety of industries and increased employment opportunities. Concern for the residents' quality of life in Curitiba is illustrated by city regulations that require, for example, that permits be obtained for cutting or pruning trees and that for every tree cut, two must be planted. A city government program allows residents to trade garbage for food, thereby supporting nearby villages and ensuring a cleaner urban center. Curitiba recycles 70 percent of its paper and 60 percent of its plastic, metals and glass.[4] The city also provides free medical care to its residents.

On a larger scale than Curitiba, the state of Kerala in southwestern India, with an area of about 15,000 square miles (38,863 square kilometers) and a population of approximately 32 million, represents an alternative model that supports low consumption and a high quality of life.[5] With a life expectancy of 72 years; one of the lowest infant mortality rates in the developing world; a population growth of 1.7 births per woman (lower than the US and Sweden); and a 90 percent literacy rate (similar to that of Singapore and Spain), Kerala approaches Western standards of living at a fractional gross domestic per capita income of just $1,000 per year (lower than that of Cambodia and Sudan).[6] How can this be?

The impressive health and education standards and freedom in governance in Kerala stand as proof that a high quality of life need not depend on material wealth. A history of social reform programs has instilled a sense of active democratic participation and established a legacy of equitable distribution of resources. Although Kerala does not exist in isolation and must face the problems of an economic system linked to the rest of India, it still manages to challenge us to reevaluate our assumptions about the link between economic development and standard of living.

In an increasingly urbanized world, these examples at the village, city and regional levels illustrate a range of approaches and opportunities for transforming sustainability principles into practical solutions.

Our General Predicament

The dawn of the new millennium is marked by both an extraordinary economic productivity and an alarming decline in the viability of the ecosystems at the foundation of our survival. We find ourselves at a time of tremendous advancements in: space technology, including the Hubble telescope, the international space station and space probes; global telecommunications networks such as the Internet and wireless technology; medicine, including new disease treatments, the mapping of the human genome and stem cell research; and nanotechnology. However, our modern lifestyle relies on the health of ecosystems that are being stretched beyond their limits. The impact of our activities is reflected in issues ranging from global climate change to species extinction.

According to Worldwatch Institute, the trends contributing to our situation include "population growth, rising temperature, falling water tables, shrinking cropland per person, collapsing fisheries, shrinking forests, and the loss of plant and animal species."[7]

Of these trends, stabilizing the first two, population and temperature, is pivotal to making progress on all other fronts:

> The overriding challenges facing our global civilization as the new century begins are to stabilize climate

and stabilize population. Success on these two fronts would make other challenges, such as reversing the deforestation of Earth, stabilizing water tables, and protecting plant and animal diversity, much more manageable. If we cannot stabilize climate and we cannot stabilize population, there is not an ecosystem on Earth that we can save. Everything will change. If developing countries cannot stabilize their populations soon, many of them face the prospect of wholesale ecosystem collapse.[8]

The optimistic side of this dire situation is that the solutions for both climate and population stabilization already exist: the former by shifting from fossil fuels to alternative energy sources such as hydrogen, solar, wind and geothermal, and the latter, even though there is considerable sociocultural resistance, by implementing reproductive services and education programs for women in developing countries.[9] The lack of political will has made for slow progress in these areas.

Sustainability offers the possibility of bringing social change values into the mainstream and pushing the mainstream toward sustainable practices. Some encouraging changes are beginning to shape our new path.

The Sustainability Revolution is in an optimal position to provide the context for dialogue and act as a catalyst for action. Sustainability provides a common language that links the central issues confronting our civilization. As an organizing principle, sustainability reflects the fundamental relationships that underlie ecological, economic and social concerns. It offers the possibility of bringing social change values into the mainstream and pushing the mainstream toward sustainable practices. Some encouraging changes are beginning to shape our new path.

Seeking an Alternative Path

The Sustainability Revolution would benefit from the promotion of solution-oriented programs with clear and tangible results. For example, sustainable programs in business must demonstrate economic advantages. Pragmatic tools such as The Natural Step, ecological audits and Life Cycle Assessment have proved themselves by helping companies save money while safeguarding the environment. Tax credits such as rebates for fuel-efficient automobiles and solar energy systems also provide incentives for wise resource use and waste reduction as does holding companies accountable for the complete life cycle of their products.

Another way to promote sustainability is to demonstrate its social advantages. In the developed nations, reducing stress and isolation and increasing family time are some of the desires of people engulfed by the demands of a fast-paced technological society. In developing nations, basic needs such as food, clean drinking water, housing and healthcare are of paramount importance for a significant portion of the population. Exchanges in appropriate technology and environmental restoration programs between the industrialized nations and their developing counterparts are imperative for improving people's lives and maintaining healthy ecosystems.

Quality of life provides a viable ethical guideline for policymakers in both the developed and developing worlds. The challenge of measuring our quality of life begins by reevaluating the assessment tools currently in use. We need to shift away from flawed economic indicators such as gross domestic product (GDP), which fails to distinguish between monetary transactions that enhance and those that degrade our well-being, to tools such as the Human Development Index, the Living Planet Index, the Economic and Social Well-being Index and the Genuine Progress Indicator (GPI). These indicators more accurately account for factors that enhance human and environmental well-being by creating community ties and protecting the planet's life-support systems including clean air, clean water and healthy soils. The GPI, for example, takes into account the value of household work, parenting tasks and volunteer work. Unlike GDP, the GPI subtracts costs associated with degrading our well-being such as crime, traffic accidents and pollution.[10]

The Netherlands' green plan, NEPP4, has adopted the theme of quality of life as a basis for making decisions. The highly industrialized Dutch culture lends an important insight to developing nations aspiring to reach a comparable standard of living. The Dutch experience establishes a role model of an industrial society's commitment to maintaining its economic viability while at the same time taking responsibility for ecological needs. The Dutch also address social equity concerns through policies that maintain a relatively low disparity in the income distribution of its citizens.

While NEPP4 defines "quality of life" as individuals seeking survival and a healthy, meaningful life, sustainability requires taking individual responsibility for our actions on a broad range of issues:

> All humans seek to survive, to live healthily and to live meaningfully. This still does not add up to a sustainable life, however. A sustainable life involves more: a realization, for example, that humans are not the only living creatures on the planet and must respect all life. And it involves, for example, the shouldering of responsibilities in a range of different roles: as citizen, as producer, as consumer or as citizen of the world. By bearing responsibility for the social, economic and ecological consequences of our actions both now and later, in the Netherlands and elsewhere, we will bring sustainable development closer.[11]

The diversity of cultures and perspectives from around the world highlights the importance of metaphors for inspiring people to rally around sustainable values.[12] Creative metaphors help us visualize and understand complex sustainability issues. The human body serves as a powerful metaphor for connecting us to the Earth. In the Tibetan culture, the body's veins and arteries are associated with streams and rivers. When one pollutes a river, one is in essence pol-luting one's own blood supply. This analogy makes clear that what we do to the Earth we do to ourselves.

One of the most promising strategies in environmental conser-vation is a program to identify and protect areas of high biological diversity, or biological hot spots. Twenty-five areas around the globe, representing 1.4 percent of the Earth's land surface, contain 44 per-cent of all plants, 35 percent of non-fish vertebrates and 60 percent of all terrestrial species.[13] Conservation International, the Moore Foundation and other organizations have teamed up to protect hot spots in places such as Madagascar, Indonesia, Brazil's Atlantic forest and Southeast Asia.[14] Although the hot-spot strategy is a significant first step, the long-term health of these protected zones may depend upon their integration within a broader conservation program.

Numerous consulting firms and institutes are providing innova-tive tools and solutions for companies and government agencies worldwide in search of sustainability strategies. For example, Natural Capitalism Solutions, a nonprofit organization founded by visionary Hunter Lovins, seeks to educate business, civil society and govern-ment leaders about the principles of sustainability and Natural Capitalism. Derived from the landmark book, *Natural Capitalism*, by Hunter Lovins, Amory Lovins and Paul Hawken, the Natural Capitalism principles include: Radical Resource Efficiency (increas-ing productivity of resources including energy, water, materials and people); Design for Sustainability (using nature's wisdom for innovative design approaches such as Biomimicry and Cradle to Cradle); and Manage for Prosperity and Sustainability (using Sustainable Manage-ment practices to promote greater resource efficiency and effective-ness, and restore, enhance and sustain human and natural capital).[15]

The Savory Center, an international nonprofit founded in 1984 by wildlife biologist Allan Savory, has developed the Holistic Management® Model, an innovative decision-making framework that allows people regardless of their location, industry or circum-stances to make decisions that are environmentally, socially and financially sound. With its roots in land, agriculture and wildlife management, Holistic Management provides a proactive approach for making decisions based on a holistic goal that simultaneously considers economic, social and environmental issues.[16]

Catherine Austin Fitts, founder of Solari, an investment consulting company, aims to "make healthy local living economies the best investment worldwide" through community-based, environmentally friendly and socially responsible investment programs.[17] Similarly, dozens of other consulting groups are working with corporations, small businesses and local, state and federal government departments in search of a new vision that addresses environmental and social concerns.

Beyond Green: A New Vision of the Future

Another way to expand the effectiveness of the Sustainability Revolution is to build on the alliances of other social change movements. Historically, successful mobilizations such as the civil rights, peace, and nuclear freeze movements established alliances of diverse groups with a common interest. Since the late 1990s, there has been a remarkable alliance between the labor and environmental movements.

This "blue/green" alliance demonstrated its broad support and gained the attention of international institutions by voicing its opposition to policies of the World Trade Organization (WTO), starting with the meeting in Seattle in November, 1999, and the International Monetary Fund (IMF) and the World Bank (WB) in April, 2000. This alliance has maintained its influence at subsequent meetings held by these global institutions.

The alliance of environment and labor can be expanded to other groups, including business, government and education. The tremendous marketing power of corporations that creates mass appeal for soft drinks, toys, fast food and music could do wonders for sustainable values, for example by promoting environmental restoration and education as well as green products and services. The worldwide model of Niketown centers, which currently promote a wide range of clothing products, could be adopted by sustainability groups to showcase sustainable technologies.

An encouraging initiative in the business sector is the commitment by seven companies, including DuPont, Shell and BP Amoco, to reduce greenhouse gases to 15 percent below their 1990 levels by 2010.[18] Thirty-eight other large companies have energy and greenhouse gas emission reduction programs. Additionally, in the next ten years the Green Power Market Development Group, formed by multinationals such as DuPont, GM and IBM, plans to develop markets for a thousand megawatts of renewable energy.[19]

The United Nations Global Compact, signed (albeit hesitantly) in 2000 by 50 multinationals and 12 labor and watchdog groups, legitimizes sustainability concerns. The compact has a network of almost 2,000 companies in over 70 countries and forges a commitment from corporations such as Bayer, DuPont, DaimlerChrysler, Nike and Royal Dutch Shell to work in partnership to address human rights, labor and ecological issues.[20]

Local government measures such as San Francisco's 2001 Solar Revenue Bond, which with the H Bond will generate $100 million for the installation of solar power, wind power and energy efficient technologies on city buildings, have set the stage for innovative government actions that promote renewable energy. Through solar installations on public buildings, San Francisco hopes to generate 10 megawatts in the first five years and eventually an additional 40 megawatts, or enough power to meet about five percent of the city's peak electricity needs.[21] These bonds are paid for by energy savings, thereby eliminating any tax increase. Over a dozen other US cities, including San Diego, Denver and New York, are looking into following a similar path toward renewable energy solutions.

In the political arena, the German Green party's success in the 1980s in capturing the people's concern for sustainability issues points to the benefits of a more flexible, inclusive platform willing to work with other sectors of society. By moderately emphasizing economic and social in addition to ecological factors, the Green party might gain wider support for its values in international political circles.

All these alliances indicate a shift of sustainability issues from the periphery into the mainstream, where they now are becoming influential in the world of politics, labor and commerce.

Although there has been a recent increase of innovative environmental education programs at colleges and universities (e.g., Brown, Tufts, Yale, College of the Atlantic, Antioch College, Colorado College, Middlebury College, New College of California, Oberlin College), a more integrated curriculum of sustainability (including themes related to ecology, economy and equity) has yet to be widely adopted by educational institutions.[22]

The Talloires Declaration, with over 300 signatory institutions in more than 40 countries, is a useful framework for colleges and universities to adopt as a first step in promoting ecoliteracy and sustainability education initiatives.[23] An interdisciplinary educational approach establishing sustainability as the context for all learning would enhance understanding of our interdependence with the Earth.

Remarkable human achievements in the eradication of diseases such as smallpox point to the success of a unified vision backed by international cooperation. The 1987 Montreal Protocol on Substances that Deplete the Ozone Layer represents a similar undertaking —a commitment by the world community to phasing out chlorofluorocarbons (CFCs), halons, carbon tetrachloride and methyl chloroform, which deplete the ozone layer that protects life on Earth from damaging ultraviolet radiation exposure. In addition, the long-awaited approval of the Kyoto Protocol by Russia, along with the treaty's ratification by 120 other nations (excluding the US), is a milestone for the international community as the first collective step toward curbing global warming.

Success requires an understanding of the complex forces at work, a vision of the future and a strategy for making the vision a reality.

The significance of these efforts lies in the effectiveness of awareness coupled with action. Success requires an understanding of the complex forces at work, a vision of the future and a strategy for making the vision a reality. The shocking terrorist attacks of September 11, 2001 prompted many people to embark on a profound reassessment of their life values and purpose. Now, at this pivotal time of unprecedented change, each and every one of us faces a responsibility for acting on a shared vision of a sustainable future. Like the Aboriginal Songlines, which act as both land ethic and compass, the principles of sustainability will guide us through the choices we must make.

Resources

For regularly updated resource information, please visit
www.sustainabilityrevolution.com

Organizations (in their own words)

Sustainability overview

Bioneers
Website: www.bioneers.org
Founded in 1990, Bioneers is a nonprofit organization that promotes
practical environmental solutions and innovative social strategies for
restoring the Earth and its communities.

The Buckminster Fuller Institute
Website: www.bfi.org
The Buckminster Fuller Institute is committed to a successful and
sustainable future for 100% of humanity. Founded in 1983 and
inspired by the Design Science principles pioneered by the late
Buckminster Fuller, BFI serves as an information resource for concerned citizens around the world.

Center for a New American Dream
Website: www.newdream.org
The Center for a New American Dream is a not-for-profit organization dedicated to helping individuals and institutions reduce and
shift consumption to enhance quality of life and protect the environment. We are building a strong network of organizations and
individuals to promote sustainable policies and practices that will
ensure a healthy planet for future generations.

The Center for Ecoliteracy
Website: www.ecoliteracy.org
The Center for Ecoliteracy was founded in 1995 by Fritjof Capra, Peter Buckley, and Zenobia Barlow to foster the experience and understanding of the natural world. The Center is a public non-profit foundation that supports a network of Northern California grantees, many of which are schools and educational organizations engaged in habitat restoration and agriculturally-related programs, such as school gardens and food systems.

Chaordic Commons
Website: www.chaordic.org
...To develop, disseminate and implement new concepts of organization that result in more equitable sharing of power and wealth, improved health, and greater compatibility with the human spirit and biosphere.

The Citizens Network for Sustainable Development
Website: www.citnet.org
The Citizens Network for Sustainable Development (CitNet) is an independent, nonprofit network bringing together US based organizations, communities, and individuals working on sustainability issues across the US. CitNet works in the local, regional, and global arenas to make sustainable development a reality.

Conservation Economy.net
Website: www.conservationeconomy.net
On this site, fifty-seven patterns provide a framework for an ecologically restorative, socially just, and reliably prosperous society. They are adaptable to local ecosystems and cultures, yet universal in their applicability. Together they form what we call a Conservation Economy.

David Suzuki Foundation
Website: www.davidsuzuki.org
Since 1990, the David Suzuki Foundation has worked to find ways

for society to live in balance with the natural world that sustains us. Focusing on four program areas — oceans and sustainable fishing, forests and wild lands, climate change and clean energy, and the web of life — the Foundation uses science and education to promote solutions that help conserve nature.

Earth Policy Institute
Website: www.earth-policy.org
The goal of the Earth Policy Institute is to raise public awareness to the point where it will support an effective public response to the threats posed by continuing population growth, rising CO_2 emissions, the loss of plant and animal species, and the many other trends that are adversely affecting the Earth. The dissemination of information from the Institute is designed to help set the public agenda.

Ecotrust
Website: www.ecotrust.org
Ecotrust was created in 1991 by a small group of diverse people who sought to bring some of the good ideas emerging around sustainability back to the rain forests of home. We set out to characterize this region [between Alaska and Northern California] and articulate a more enduring strategy for its prosperity.

Education for Sustainability Western Network
Website: www.efswest.org
The Education for Sustainability Western Network ("EFS West") is a professional association of individuals and institutions working to make sustainability integral to higher education in the western US and Canada. The Network was founded in 2001 as a partnership with Second Nature.

E.F. Schumacher Society
Website: www.schumachersociety.org
The E. F. Schumacher Society, named after the author of *Small Is*

Beautiful: Economics As If People Mattered, is an educational non-profit organization founded in 1980. Our programs demonstrate that both social and environmental sustainability can be achieved by applying the values of human-scale communities and respect for the natural environment to economic issues. Building on a rich tradition often known as decentralism, the Society initiates practical measures that lead to community revitalization and further the transition toward an economically and ecologically sustainable society.

Forum on Religion and Ecology
Website: http://environment.harvard.edu/religion
The Forum on Religion and Ecology is the largest international multireligious project of its kind. With its conferences, publications, and website it is engaged in exploring religious worldviews, texts, and ethics in order to broaden understanding of the complex nature of current environmental concerns.

HORIZON International
Website: www.yale.edu/horizon
HORIZON International is a not-for-profit international research, film production and development organization founded in 1976 and dedicated to furthering solutions to environmental, health, population and development problems.

International Institute for Sustainable Development
Website: http://iisd.ca
For development to be sustainable it must integrate environmental stewardship, economic development and the well-being of all people — not just for today but for countless generations to come. This is the challenge facing governments, non-governmental organizations, private enterprises, communities and individuals. The International Institute for Sustainable Development meets this challenge by advancing policy recommendations on international trade and investment, economic policy, climate change, measurement and indicators, and natural resource management to make development sustainable.

The International Society for Ecological Economics
Website: www.ecoeco.org
The Society facilitates understanding between economists and ecologists and the integration of their thinking into a transdiscipline aimed at developing a sustainable world.

The Jane Goodall Institute
Website: www.janegoodall.org
Founded by renowned primatologist Jane Goodall, JGI is a global nonprofit that empowers people to make a difference for all living things. We are creating healthy ecosystems, promoting sustainable livelihoods, and nurturing new generations of committed, active citizens around the world.

ManyOne Networks
Website: www.manyone.net
ManyOne Networks combines a breakthrough web browser with an ad-free Internet service offering Internet users a compelling, world-class option to the over-commercialized Internet services available today. In conjunction with the browser and its service, ManyOne will promote the creation of a digital commons called the Digital Universe, an immersive experience unlike anything else available on the web today.

Natural Capitalism Solutions
Website: www.natcapsolutions.org
Natural Capitalism Solutions (NCS) is a nonprofit organization that educates decision-makers in business, civil society and government about the principles of sustainability, Natural Capitalism and the opportunities to achieve genuine progress through its implementation.

New Dimensions
Website: www.newdimensions.org
New Dimensions Broadcasting Network is a communications medium like no other. An independent, listener-supported producer

and distributor of public radio and shortwave programs, New Dimensions is dedicated to presenting a diversity of views from many traditions and cultures, and strives to impart practical knowledge and perennial wisdom. New Dimensions fosters the process of living a more healthy life of mind, body and spirit while deepening our connections to self, family, community and the environment.

OneWorld.net
Website: www.oneworld.net
OneWorld is the world's favourite and fastest-growing civil society network online, supporting people's media to help build a more just global society.

Planet Ark
Website: www.planetark.org
Planet Ark's aim is to show people and business the many ways that they can reduce their day to day impact on the environment. It's an Australian not-for-profit organisation that was set up by the tennis player Pat Cash and international charity campaigner Jon Dee back in June 1991.

Planetwork
Website: www.planetwork.net
Planetwork explores how the creative application of digital tools — visualization technologies, software, and the Internet, among others — can open new possibilities for positive global change.

Rocky Mountain Institute
Website: www.rmi.org
Rocky Mountain Institute (RMI), a 501(c)(3) nonprofit organization, was established in 1982 by resource analysts L. Hunter Lovins and Amory B. Lovins. What began as a small group of colleagues focusing on energy policy has since grown into a broad-based institution with approximately forty full-time staff, an annual budget of nearly $6 million (over half of it earned through programmatic

enterprise), and a global reach. RMI brings a unique perspective to resource issues, guided by the following core principles: Advanced Resource Productivity; Systems Thinking; Positive Action; Market-Oriented Solutions; End-Use/Least-Cost Approach; Biological Insight; Corporate Transformation; The Pursuit of Interconnections; Natural Capitalism.

Second Nature: Education for Sustainability
Website: www.secondnature.org
Since 1993, Second Nature has been dedicated to accelerating a process of transformation in higher education. We chose to assist colleges and universities in their quest to integrate sustainability as a core component of all education and practice, and to help expand their efforts to make human activity sustainable.

Sristi
Website: www.sristi.org
Sristi is a non-governmental organisation setup to strengthen the creativity of grassroots inventors, innovators and ecopreneurs engaged in conserving biodiversity and developing eco-friendly solutions to local problems. Here, on the official web site of Sristi, you can read about its activities and participate in them, download its newsletter and research papers and much more.

Sustainability Institute
Website: www.sustainer.org
The Sustainability Institute provides information, analysis, and practical demonstrations that can foster transitions to sustainable systems at all levels of society, from local to global.

The Sustainability Web Ring
Website: http://sdgateway.net/webring/default.htm
Welcome to the Sustainability Web Ring, a service of the SD Gateway. This Internet tool allows users to navigate easily between web sites that deal with the principles, policies, and best practices for

sustainable development. By following the links through the web ring, you will find information from around the world on how to deal with such crucial issues as: climate change, cleaner production, waste, poverty, consumerism, natural resource management, and governance. This information is particularly suited to decision-makers within civil society, government, business, research and funding institutions, and communities.

United Nations Environment Network

Website: www.unep.net

Welcome to UNEP.Net, the United Nations Environment Network: a global portal to authoritative environmental information based on themes and regions.

The World Café

Website: www.theworldcafe.com

World Café Conversations are an intentional way to create a living network of conversation around questions that matter. A Café Conversation is a creative process for leading collaborative dialogue, sharing knowledge and creating possibilities for action in groups of all sizes.

World Resources Institute

Website: www.wri.org

World Resources Institute is an independent nonprofit organization with a staff of more than 100 scientists, economists, policy experts, business analysts, statistical analysts, mapmakers, and communicators working to protect the Earth and improve people's lives.

Worldwatch Institute

Website: www.worldwatch.org

The Worldwatch Institute is dedicated to fostering the evolution of an environmentally sustainable society — one in which human needs are met in ways that do not threaten the health of the natural environment or the prospects of future generations. The Institute seeks to achieve this goal through the conduct of inter-disciplinary non-partisan research on emerging global environmental issues, the results of which are widely disseminated throughout the world.

The World Wide Web Virtual Library:
Sustainable Development
Website: www.ulb.ac.be/ceese/meta/sustvl.html
A comprehensive list of internet sites dealing with sustainable development, including organisations, projects and activities, electronic journals, libraries, references and documents, databases, directories or metadatabases.

Wuppertal Institute for Climate, Environment, and Energy
Website: www.wupperinst.org
The Wuppertal Institute explores and develops environmental policy guidelines, strategies and instruments in order to promote sustainability at the regional, national and international level.

Zero Emissions Research and Initiatives (ZERI)
Website: http://zeri.org
Zero Emissions Research & Initiatives (ZERI) is a global network of creative minds seeking solutions to world challenges. The common vision shared by the members of the ZERI family is to view waste as resource and seek solutions using nature's design principles as inspiration.

Sustainability and community

Global Footprint Network
Website: www.footprintnetwork.net
The Global Footprint Network is committed to fostering a world where all people have the opportunity to live satisfying lives within the means of Earth's ecological capacity. We are dedicated to advancing the scientific rigor and practical application of the Ecological Footprint, a tool that quantifies human demand on nature, and nature's capacity to meet these demands.

The Globalist
Website: www.theglobalist.com
The Globalist is a daily online feature service that covers the biggest story of our lifetime — globalization. Our business has for-profit and nonprofit components: Besides maintaining a public website, we offer a variety of licensing, syndication and sponsorship options to interested clients and partners. Our publication partners are global companies, international organizations, high schools, colleges, newspapers and magazines, radio stations — and foundations.

ICLEI
Website: www.iclei.org
ICLEI — Local Governments for Sustainability was founded in 1990 by local governments at the United Nations Headquarters in New York as the International Council for Local Environmental Initiatives. Its mission is to build and serve a worldwide movement of local governments to achieve tangible improvements in global sustainability with special focus on environmental conditions through cumulative local actions.

International Forum on Globalization
Website: www.ifg.org
The International Forum on Globalization (IFG) is an alliance of sixty leading activists, scholars, economists, researchers and writers formed to stimulate new thinking, joint activity, and public education in response to economic globalization.

International Society for Ecology and Culture
Website: www.isec.org.uk
The International Society for Ecology and Culture (ISEC) is a nonprofit organisation concerned with the protection of both biological and cultural diversity. Our emphasis is on education for action: moving beyond single issues to look at the more fundamental influences that shape our lives.

Redefining Progress
Website: www.rprogress.org

Redefining Progress (RP) works with a broad array of partners to shift the economy and public policy towards sustainability.

Resource Renewal Institute
Website: www.rri.org
The Resource Renewal Institute (RRI) is a nonprofit organization dedicated to solving complex environmental problems by developing, promoting and facilitating innovative strategies for a sustainable future.

Smart Communities Network
Website: www.sustainable.doe.gov
We are delighted to offer you this menu of information and services on how your community can adopt sustainable development as a strategy for well-being. You'll be in good company. We're finding that more and more cities, villages, neighborhoods and regions are using sustainable development as a guiding principle not only for near-term projects, but also for planning their futures.

Sustainable Communities Network
Website: www.sustainable.org
Linking citizens to resources and to one another to create healthy, vital and sustainable communities.

Sustainable Seattle
Website: www.sustainableseattle.org
Founded in 1991, Sustainable Seattle is a non-profit organization dedicated to enhancing the long term quality of life in the Seattle / King County area.

Sustainability and commerce

AtKisson, Inc.
Website: www.atkisson.com
AtKisson, Inc. is an international network of professional consultants, trainers, facilitators, researchers, writers and designers, with bases in

the US, Europe, and Australia; and with strategic relationships with a number of other firms and organizations around the world.

Business for Social Responsibility
Website: www.bsr.org
Business for Social Responsibility is a membership organization for companies of all sizes and sectors. BSR's mission is to be the leading global resource providing members with innovative products and services that help companies be commercially successful in ways that demonstrate respect for ethical values, people, communities, and the environment.

Clean Edge, Inc.
Website: www.cleanedge.com
Clean Edge, Inc., based in the San Francisco Bay Area, is a research and strategic marketing firm that helps companies, investors, policy-makers, and nonprofits understand and profit from clean-energy technologies. Through its research reports and publications, strategic marketing services, and co-sponsored conferences and events, Clean Edge's mission is to accurately track clean-energy trends and identify market opportunities.

Coalition for Environmentally Responsible Economies
Website: www.ceres.org
CERES is a nonprofit coalition of investors, public pension funds, foundations, labor unions and environmental, religious and public interest groups working in partnership with companies toward the common goal of corporate environmental responsibility worldwide.

EcoSTEPS
Website: www.ecosteps.com.au
EcoSTEPS is a multi-disciplinary consultancy providing specialised services to people in organisations seeking to operate and interact in ways that contribute to a sustainable world. We provide support and advice to a broad range of organisations across all sectors of society.

We are based in Sydney, Australia with associates and connections throughout Australia, New Zealand, UK and the USA.

GreenBiz.com

Website: http://greenbiz.com

The nonprofit, nonpartisan GreenBiz.com works to harness the power of technology to bring environmental information, resources, and tools to the mainstream business community. Its principal mission is: "To provide clear, concise, accurate, and balanced information, resources, and learning opportunities to help companies of all sizes and sectors integrate environmental responsibility into their operations in a manner that combines ecological sustainability with profitable business practices."

Media Venture Collective

Website: www.mediaventure.org

Media Venture Collective is a donor-advised fund of the Rudolf Steiner Foundation, administered collaboratively with the Calvert Foundation. It is a hybrid between a community foundation and a venture fund. It invests strategically and aggressively like the latter, applying profits to new projects to expand the fund's assets, with two fundamental differences: 1) its focus is on helping citizen-based independent media thrive; and 2) the funds come from grants and donations, not from investors expecting financial returns.

National Strategies for Sustainable Development

Website: www.nssd.net

This web site provides tools to assist in promoting dialogues on national strategies for sustainable development and providing necessary background information and reference material in support of these dialogues.

Natural Capitalism, Inc.

Website: www.natcapinc.com

Natural Capitalism, Inc. (NCI) is a Boulder-based company that helps business, governments, academic institutions, and international communities become simultaneously more profitable and environmentally/socially sustainable. NCI was founded in September 2003; its sister organization, Natural Capitalism Solutions, a nonprofit, was founded in 2004. Hunter Lovins, a world-renowned leader in sustainability policy and strategies, is founder and president of both organizations.

Natural Logic, Inc.
Website: www.natlogic.com
Natural Logic, Inc. delivers internet-based decision support software, strategic consulting, management training, workshops, and related business services that help companies turn exceptional environmental performance into competitive advantage. The US economy produces only 6% product, and 94% non-product. Our job is to help companies reverse that ratio, moving toward zero waste and 100% product.

The Natural Step
Website: www.naturalstep.ca
The Natural Step (TNS) is an international nonprofit organization based in 12 different countries that uses a science-based systems framework to help organizations, individuals, and communities take steps toward sustainability. The mission of TNS is to catalyze systemic change and make fundamental principles of sustainability easier to understand, and meaningful sustainability initiatives easier to implement.

SocialFunds.com
Website: www.socialfunds.com
SocialFunds.com is a website of SRI World Group, Inc., a news, research, and consulting firm that advises clients regarding sustainability investment issues and corporate responsibility practices.

Social Investment Forum
Website: www.socialinvest.org
A national nonprofit membership organization promoting the concept, practice and growth of socially responsible investing.

SustainAbility
Website: www.sustainability.com
Founded in 1987, SustainAbility is the longest established international consultancy specializing in business strategy and sustainable development — environmental improvement, social equity and economic development.

SustainableBusiness.com
Website: www.sustainablebusiness.com
We use the Internet to "grease the wheels" — to accelerate the spread of sustainable business practices by increasing market penetration of sustainable products, services, and the companies that produce them. SB.com covers the field as a whole, bringing together businesses from such diverse industries as renewable energy, organic products, social investing, green building and construction, and re-manufacturing.

Sustainability and natural resources

Ag BioTech InfoNet
Website: www.biotech-info.net
Ag BioTech InfoNet covers all aspects of the application of biotechnology and genetic engineering in agricultural production and food processing and marketing. Our focus is on scientific reports and findings and technical analysis, although the page also covers emerging issues of widespread interest, developments in the policy arena, and major media coverage.

AgNIC
Website: www.agnic.org
The AgNIC (Agriculture Network Information Center) Alliance began in 1995 with land-grant institutions and the National Agricultural Library committed to a partnership to provide access to quality information and resources over the Internet.

The Center for Food Safety
Website: www.centerforfoodsafety.org

The Center for Food Safety (CFS) is a nonprofit public interest and environmental advocacy membership organization established in 1997 by its sister organization, International Center for Technology Assessment, for the purpose of challenging harmful food production technologies and promoting sustainable alternatives.

Forests.org
Website: http://forests.org
Forests.org works to end deforestation, preserve primary and old-growth forests, conserve and sustainably manage other forests, conserve water and climatic systems and commence the age of ecological restoration.

Forest Stewardship Council
Website: www.fsc.org
The Forest Stewardship Council (FSC) is an independent, not-for-profit, non-government organisation based in Bonn, Germany, that provides standard setting, trademark assurance and accreditation services for companies and organisations interested in responsible forestry.

Institute for Sustainable Forestry
Website: www.isf-sw.org
The Institute for Sustainable Forestry promotes sustainable forest management that contributes to the long-term ecological, economic, and social well-being of forest based communities in the Pacific Northwest.

The Land Institute
Website: www.landinstitute.org
When people, land, and community are as one, all three members prosper; when they relate not as members but as competing interests, all three are exploited. By consulting Nature as the source and measure of that membership, The Land Institute seeks to develop an agriculture that will save soil from being lost or poisoned while promoting a community life at once prosperous and enduring.

The Leopold Center for Sustainable Agriculture

Website: www.leopold.iastate.edu

The Leopold Center is a research and education center with statewide programs to develop sustainable agricultural practices that are both profitable and conserve natural resources. It was established under the Groundwater Protection Act of 1987 with a three-fold mission: to conduct research into the negative impacts of agricultural practices; to assist in developing alternative practices; to work with ISU [Iowa State University] Extension to inform the public of Leopold Center findings.

NOAA Fisheries

Website: www.nmfs.noaa.gov

NOAA Fisheries is the federal agency, a division of the Department of Commerce, responsible for the stewardship of the nation's living marine resources and their habitat. NOAA Fisheries is responsible for the management, conservation and protection of living marine resources within the United States' Exclusive Economic Zone (water 3 to 200 mile[s] offshore).

Rainforest Action Network

Website: www.ran.org

Rainforest Action Network campaigns for the forests, their inhabitants and the natural systems that sustain life by transforming the global marketplace through grassroots organizing, education and non-violent direct action.

Salmon Nation

Website: www.salmonnation.org

Welcome to a community of caretakers and citizens, a community that stretches across arbitrary boundaries and bridges urban-rural divides. We bring new meaning to the word cooperative — with unusual alliances of tribes, fishermen, farmers, loggers, and urban-dwellers working together to improve our neighborhoods and watersheds.

Sustainable Fisheries Foundation
Website: www.sff.bc.ca
The Sustainable Fisheries Foundation is a nonprofit organization dedicated to the protection, enhancement and wise use of fisheries resources in the Pacific Northwest. Our mission is to promote a balanced approach to fisheries management — one based on sound ecological and economic principles — to ensure that fish populations remain viable, productive and accessible to future generations.

Sustainability and ecological design

Architects/Designers/Planners for Social Responsibility
Website: www.adpsr.org
ADPSR believes design practitioners have a significant role to play in the well-being of our communities. The goal of our programs is to 1) raise professional and public awareness of critical social and environmental issues; 2) further responsive design and planning; and 3) honor persons and organizations whose work exemplifies social responsibility.

Builders Without Borders
Website: www.builderswithoutborders.org
We are an international network of ecological builders who form partnerships with communities and organizations around the world to create affordable housing from local materials and to work together for a sustainable future. We believe the solution to homelessness is not merely housing, but a local population trained to provide housing for themselves.

Building Green, Inc.
Website: www.buildinggreen.com
We are an independent company committed to providing accurate, unbiased, and timely information designed to help building-industry professionals and policy makers improve the environmental performance, and reduce the adverse impacts, of buildings. We offer

both print and electronic resources to help you design and build construction projects from a whole-systems perspective and take an integrated design approach that minimizes ecological impact and maximizes economic performance. We are the publishers of *Environmental Building News.*

Cradle2Cradle

Website: www.cradle2cradle.org

This site is maintained by Earth Care International, a nonprofit organization. The purpose is to educate the general public about the concepts behind cradle-to-cradle (c2c). This site is a resource to implement these concepts in the businesses that you work for and buy from. Cradle2Cradle.org is your complete source for who is doing what and how you can participate.

Ecological Design Institute

Website: www.ecodesign.org/cdi

The Ecological Design Institute and Van der Ryn Architects create innovative design solutions that link nature, culture and technology to reintegrate the needs of human society within the balance of nature.

GreenBlue

Website: www.greenblue.org

GreenBlue acts as a catalyst to transform the making of things ... encouraging and enabling the widespread adoption and implementation of sustainable thinking and design. We provide the theoretical, technical, and information tools required to transform industry into an economically profitable, ecologically regenerative, and socially empowering activity through intelligent design.

Living Machines

Website: www.livingmachines.com

Living Machines (LM), a division of Dharma Living Systems, Inc., designs ecologically engineered natural wastewater treatment and reclamation systems for a broad spectrum of uses.

The Product-Life Institute, Geneva

Website: www.product-life.org

The Product-Life Institute in Geneva is an independent institute which lives exclusively from contract research (studies, in-house seminars, teaching workshops and conference contributions), i.e. from selling our knowledge and time. The researchers of the institute work together or independently in their function as consultants to industrial companies, government authorities and universities. Our main focus is to develop innovative strategies and policies to foster the move towards a more sustainable society, for both industry and government.

Renewable Energy Policy Project

Website: http://solstice.crest.org

REPP's goal is to accelerate the use of renewable energy by providing credible information, insightful policy analysis, and innovative strategies amid changing energy markets and mounting environmental needs by researching, publishing, and disseminating information, creating policy tools, and hosting highly active, on-line, renewable energy discussion groups.

Sustainable Buildings Industry Council

Website: www.psic.org

SBIC is an independent, nonprofit organization whose mission is to advance the design, affordability, energy performance, and environmental soundness of residential, institutional, and commercial buildings nationwide.

US Green Building Council

Website: www.usgbc.org

The Council is the nation's foremost coalition of leaders from across the building industry working to promote buildings that are environmentally responsible, profitable and healthy places to live and work.

Van der Ryn Architects

Website: www.vanderryn.com

Van der Ryn Architects is a leader in environmentally-friendly design and planning. For over thirty-five years, we have been creating environments which enrich the human spirit, work with natural processes and respect the beauty and vitality of nature. Our approach, ECO-LOGIC Design, is a marriage of nature and technology, using ecology as the basis for design. We work at all levels of scale to produce innovative buildings, landscapes, communities, cities and applied technologies.

William McDonough + Partners

Website: www.mcdonough.com

At William McDonough + Partners, our approach to architecture is designed to accommodate complex aesthetic, economic and performance criteria into buildings that embody ecological intelligence and intergenerational justice: elegant, affordable, safe and sustainable architecture. William McDonough founded his architecture practice in New York City in 1981. Since then his firm has taken the lead in producing designs of the highest aesthetic quality that also incorporate extraordinary environmental sensitivity.

World Green Building Council

Website: www.worldgbc.org

The WorldGBC was formed in 1999 with the goal of coordinating and advancing the work of national green building organizations, supporting the development of standards, technologies, products and projects. The WorldGBC is incorporated in New York as a US nonprofit corporation striving to help countries form national green building councils of their own by providing valuable information and resources to its affiliates and members.

Sustainability and the biosphere

Appropriate Technology Transfer for Rural Areas

Website: www.attra.org

ATTRA — National Sustainable Agriculture Information Service, funded by the US Department of Agriculture, is managed by the

National Center for Appropriate Technology. It provides information and other technical assistance to farmers, ranchers, Extension agents, educators, and others involved in sustainable agriculture in the United States.

Biomimicry
Website: www.biomimicry.org
Biomimicry is a new science that studies nature's models and then imitates or takes inspiration from these designs and processes to solve human problems, e.g., a solar cell inspired by a leaf. Biomimicry uses an ecological standard to judge the "rightness" of our innovations. After 3.8 billion years of evolution, nature has learned: What works. What is appropriate. What lasts. Biomimicry is a new way of viewing and valuing nature. It introduces an era based not on what we can extract from the natural world, but on what we can learn from it.

Foundation for Deep Ecology
Website: www.deepecology.org
The mission of the Foundation for Deep Ecology (FDE) is to support education, advocacy, and legal action on behalf of wild Nature and in opposition to the technologies and developments that are destroying the natural world.

NatureServe
Website: www.natureserve.org
NatureServe represents a network of member programs comprising 74 independent centers that collect and analyze data about the plants, animals, and ecological communities of the Western Hemisphere. Known as natural heritage programs or conservation data centers, these programs operate in all 50 US states, in 11 provinces and territories of Canada, and in many countries and territories of Latin America and the Caribbean.

The Organic Consumers Association
Website: www.organicconsumers.org

The OCA is a grassroots nonprofit public interest organization which deals with crucial issues of food safety, industrial agriculture, genetic engineering, corporate accountability, and environmental sustainability. We are the only organization in the US focused exclusively on representing the views and interests of the nation's estimated ten million organic consumers.

The Permaculture Research Institute
Website: www.permaculture.org.au
The Permaculture Research Institute (PRI), headed by Geoff Lawton, is a nonprofit organisation involved in global networking and practical training of environmental activists. It offers solutions to local and global ecological problems, and has an innovative farm design in progress. The Institute is also involved in design and consultancy work, and actively supports several aid projects around the world.

Pew Center on Global Climate Change
Website: http://pewclimate.org
The Pew Center on Global Climate Change brings together business leaders, policy makers, scientists, and other experts to bring a new approach to a complex and often controversial issue. Our approach is based on sound science, straight talk, and a belief that we can work together to protect the climate while sustaining economic growth.

The Savory Center
Website: www.holisticmanagement.org
The Savory Center is an international not-for-profit organization established in 1984 to coordinate the development of Holistic Management® worldwide. Holistic Management has helped people all over the world more effectively manage all their resources in a truly sustainable way.

Tagari Publications
Website: www.tagari.com
Mission: To publish and distribute the best in Permaculture research.

Online Publications/Newsletters/
List Servers (in their own words)

Center for Environmental Philosophy
Website: www.cep.unt.edu/default.html
This World Wide Web server is dedicated to providing access to Internet resources throughout the world which pertain to or focus on environmental ethics and environmental philosophy.

EnviroLink News Service
Website: www.envirolink.org/environews
The EnviroLink News Service is a project of the EnviroLink Network, a nonprofit organization. The primary mission of this service is to inform EnviroLink's users about the latest news and information about the global environmental movement.

Environmental Building News
Website: www.buildinggreen.com
Environmental Building News is a monthly newsletter published since 1992 featuring comprehensive, practical information on a range of topics related to sustainable design in the built environment.

Environment News Service
Website: www.ens-news.com
The Environment News Service is the original daily international wire service of the environment. Established in 1990 by Editor-in-Chief Sunny Lewis and Managing Editor Jim Crabtree, ENS is independently owned and operated. The Environment News Service exists to present late-breaking environmental news in a fair and balanced manner.

Green Clips
Website: www.greenclips.com
Welcome to GreenClips, a summary of news on sustainable building design and related government and business issues published every two weeks by email.

Green Money Journal

Website: www.greenmoneyjournal.com

Green Money Journal encourages and promotes the awareness of socially and environmentally responsible business, investing and consumer resources in publications and online.

Grist Magazine

Website: www.grist.org

Grist is an online environmental magazine ... [that] tackles environmental topics with irreverence, intelligence, and a fresh perspective. Our goal is to inform, entertain, provoke, and encourage creative thinking about environmental problems and solutions.

LOHAS Journal Online

Website: www.lohasjournal.com

Welcome to LOHAS Journal Online, your source for executive-level news and information about the rapidly growing, $227 billion Lifestyles of Health and Sustainability (LOHAS) marketplace.

MuseLetter

Website: www.museletter.com

MuseLetter's purpose is to offer a continuing critique of corporate-capitalist industrial civilization and a re-visioning of humanity's prospects for the next millennium. Subjects range from global economics to religion to the origin of humanity's antipathy toward nature. All essays are informed by a wide-ranging, interdisciplinary study of history and culture.

Permaculture Activist

Website: www.permacultureactivist.net

The Activist is North America's leading permaculture periodical offering articles on permaculture design, edible landscaping, bioregionalism, aquaculture, natural building, earthworks, renewable energy, and much more.

Permaculture Magazine

Website: www.permaculture.co.uk

Permaculture Magazine is published quarterly for enquiring minds and original thinkers everywhere. Each issue gives you practical, thought provoking articles written by leading experts as well as fantastic permaculture tips from readers!

Rachel's Environment & Health News

Website: www.rachel.org/home_eng.htm
Rachel's provides timely information on toxic substances and other environmental hazards. The newsletter covers many technical issues ... but it is written in plain language that anyone can understand ....
Rachel's tries to put environmental problems into a political context of money and power, so that people can see how all our problems ... are connected.

Resurgence Magazine Online

Website: http://resurgence.gn.apc.org
Resurgence is the leading international forum for ecological and spiritual thinking, where you can explore the ideas of the great writers and thinkers of our time, both in print and on-line.

TIDEPOOL

Website: www.tidepool.org/home.html
TIDEPOOL is updated every weekday by nine a.m. with the best news stories collected from more than two dozen online news sources. Our goal is to provide the [Northwest US] Bioregional community with a daily source of the news they need to create a conservation based economy.

World Watch Magazine

Website: www.worldwatch.org/mag/index.html
World Watch: Working for a Sustainable Future focuses exclusively on issues that will determine the Earth's long-term health: the battle to rein in an out-of-control consumer economy, to stabilize the global climate, and to protect our rapidly declining cultural and biological diversity.

YES! Magazine

Website: http://futurenet.org

YES! is published by the Positive Futures Network, a nonprofit organization that supports people's active engagement in creating a more just, sustainable, and compassionate world.

Additional principles

Aalborg Charter

Website: www.aalborg.dk/engelsk/information+about+aalborg/aalborg+charter.htm

Ahwahnee Principles

Website: www.lgc.org/ahwahnee/principles.html

Aspen Principles

Website: www.aspeninstitute.org

Blueprint 2030

Website: www.metrocouncil.org/planning/blueprint2030/overview.htm

Caux Round Table Principles for Business

Website: www.cauxroundtable.org/principles.html

City of Portland Sustainable City Principles

Website: www.sustainableportland.org/default.asp?sec=stp&pg=sdc_principles

Declaration of Leadership

Website: www.declarationofleadership.com

Enlibra Principles

Website: www.westgov.org/wga/initiatives/enlibra/default.htm

The Gold Institute Environment, Health, and Safety Principles for Gold Mining

Website: www.goldinstitute.org/mining/environ.html#ENVIR

International Institute for Sustainable Development (list of principles)
Website: http://iisd.ca/sd/principle.asp

Silicon Principles
Website: www.svtc.org/icrt/siprinc.htm

Statement of Environmental Commitment by the Insurance Industry
Website: http://unepfi.org/signatories/statements/ii/index.html

Sustainability Principles for Water Management in Canada
Website: www.cwra.org/About_CWRA/CWRA_Policies_and_
Principals/cwra_policies_and_principals.html

Annotated Bibliography

Aberly, Doug, ed. *Boundaries of Home: Mapping for Local Empowerment*. New Society Publishers, 1993. A bioregional perspective on using maps as tools to help communities better understand the significance of their surroundings.

Alexander, Christopher. *A Vision of a Living World: The Nature of Order, Book 3*. Center for Environmental Structure, 2004. Part of a four-volume set that explores the nature of design, geometric properties, human habitation and the theory of living process with examples from projects throughout the world.

Alexander, Christopher, Sara Ishikawa and Murray Silverstein. *A Pattern Language*. Oxford University Press, 1977. Part of a comprehensive three-volume set exploring alternative perspectives on architecture, building and planning.

Allen, Robert. *How to Save the World*. Rowman and Littlefield, 1980. Based on the Global Conservation Strategy, this is one of the earliest works describing the concept of sustainability.

Anderson, Ray C. *Mid-Course Correction: Toward a Sustainable Enterprise: The Interface Model*. Peregrinzilla Press, 1998. The story of a corporate leader's experience in implementing sustainable business practices.

Andruss, Van, Christopher Plant, Judith Plant and Eleanor Wright, eds. *Home! A Bioregional Reader*. New Society Publishers, 1990. A wide-ranging collection of essays about bioregionalism.

AtKisson, Alan. *Believing Cassandra: An Optimist Looks at a Pessimist's World*. Chelsea Green Publishing Company, 1999. A positive outlook on the ecological, economic and social issues confronting the world.

Ausubel, Kenny. *Seeds of Change: The Living Treasure*. Harper-SanFrancisco, 1994. The story of a seed company and a call for the protection of biodiversity.

Ausubel, Kenny. *Restoring the Earth: Visionary Solutions from the Bioneers*. H. J. Kramer, 1997. Fascinating perspectives from leading thinkers on solving environmental problems.

Bartlett, Albert A. "Reflections on Sustainability, Population Growth, and the Environment — Revisited." *Focus*. Vol. 9, no. 1, 1999, pp. 49-68. <www.hubbertpeak.com/bartlett/reflections.htm>. A review of sustainability issues including population, carrying capacity and economic development.

Bateson, Gregory. *Steps to an Ecology of Mind: Collected Essays in Anthropology, Psychiatry, Evolution, and Epistemology*. University of Chicago Press, 2000. A fascinating exploration of the mind and our interactions with other species, our culture and the universe.

Bateson, Gregory. *Mind and Nature: A Necessary Unity*. 1979. Hampton Press, 2002. A philosophical journey into the patterns and connections of our thoughts and perceptions.

Benyus, Janine M. *Biomimicry*. William Morrow and Company, 1997. Explores the benefits of using nature as model, measure and mentor.

Bernard, Ted and Jora Young. *The Ecology of Hope*. New Society Publishers, 1997. An inspiring collection of successful ecological restoration efforts.

Berry, Thomas. *The Dream of the Earth*. Sierra Club Books, 1990. An examination of the human relationship to the natural world and the possibilities for a "biocracy" that restores the Earth.

Berry, Thomas. *The Great Work: Our Way into the Future*. Harmony/Bell Tower, 2000. A persuasive and eloquent exploration of the opportunities for creating a sustainable future.

Berry, Wendell. T*he Unsettling of America: Culture and Agriculture*. 3rd ed., University of California Press, 1996. Explores the ecological, social, economic and political impacts of the American culture's alienation from the land.

Berry, Wendell. *Life is a Miracle: An Essay Against Modern*

Superstition. Counterpoint Press, 2001. A provocative analysis of E.O. Wilson's *Consilience: The Unity of Knowledge,* the limitations of scientific knowledge and the significance of religion and art in exploring the miracle of life.

Brand, Stewart. *How Buildings Learn: What Happens After They're Built.* Penguin Books, 1995. An innovative perspective, with historical photos, on the evolution of buildings through time.

Brown, Lester R. *Building a Sustainable Society.* W.W. Norton and Company, 1981. A seminal work outlining the building blocks of a sustainable society.

Brown, Lester R. *Eco-Economy: Building an Economy for the Earth.* W.W. Norton and Company, 2001. A well-researched and well-written narrative describing the shifts in perception essential for a sustainable future.

Brown, Lester R. *Plan B: Rescuing a Planet under Stress and a Civilization in Trouble.* W.W. Norton and Company, 2003. Builds on Brown's earlier *Eco-Economy* and lucidly outlines the global environmental issues and options for alternative paths.

Brown, Lester R. *Outgrowing the Earth: The Food Security Challenge in an Age of Falling Water Tables and Rising Temperatures.* W.W. Norton and Company, 2005. An insightful review of the effects of economic and population growth and their impact on ecosystems and the world's food supply.

Capra, Fritjof. *The Turning Point: Science, Society, and the Rising Culture.* Bantam Books, 1983. A systems perspective on the transformation influencing technological, scientific and social changes.

Capra, Fritjof. *Uncommon Wisdom: Conversations with Remarkable People.* Bantam Books, 1989. Intriguing interviews with leading thinkers on social, ecological and ethical topics.

Capra, Fritjof. *The Web of Life: A New Scientific Understanding of Living Systems.* Anchor Books, 1996. A new perspective on the underlying patterns of living systems.

Capra, Fritjof. *The Hidden Connections: Integrating the Biological, Cognitive and Social Dimensions of Life into a Science of Sustainability.* Doubleday Books, 2002. Building on his past works, this book examines the relationship between scientific theories and human organizations.

Carson, Rachel. *Silent Spring*. 1962. Houghton Mifflin, 1994. This landmark work describing the effects of insecticides and pesticides shifted society's attention toward environmental consciousness.

Center for a New American Dream. *Sustainable Planet*. Beacon Press, 2003. An encouraging series of essays that present alternative ways of coping with the challenges of a fast-paced consumer society.

Chatwin, Bruce. *The Songlines*. Viking Penguin, 1987. An engaging account of encounters with the Aboriginal culture and its worldview.

Costanza, Robert. "Four Visions of the Century Ahead: Will It Be Star Trek, Ecotopia, Big Government, or Mad Max?" *The Futurist*. February 1999. An ecological economist's perspective on four future scenarios and the choices at hand.

Daily, Gretchen C., ed. *Nature's Services: Societal Dependence on Natural Ecosystems*. Island Press, 1997. Reexamines the notion of natural resources by looking at the critical role of ecological systems in providing basic life-support functions on Earth.

Daily, Gretchen C. and Katherine Ellison. *The New Economy of Nature: The Quest to Make Conservation Profitable*. Shearwater Books, 2003. Presents conservation strategies based on alternative financial models.

Dale, Ann and S.B. Hill. *At the Edge: Sustainable Development in the 21st Century*. University of British Columbia Press, Sustainability and Environment Series, 2002. A call for implementing sustainable development strategies that embrace economic, environmental and social considerations, and for strong leadership from governments at all levels.

Daly, Herman E. *Beyond Growth: The Economics of Sustainable Development*. Beacon Press, 1996. A seminal work describing the key economic considerations affecting sustainable development.

Devall, Bill and George Sessions. *Deep Ecology: Living as if Nature Mattered*. Peregrine Smith Books, Gibbs Smith Publishers, 1985. A sound description of the key concepts of deep ecology.

Durning, Alan Thein. *This Place on Earth: Home and the Practice of*

Permanence. Northwest Environment Watch, 1996. A personal account examining the challenges and opportunities of living sustainably in the Pacific Northwest.

Earth Pledge Foundation. *Sustainable Architecture White Papers: Essays on Design and Building for a Sustainable Future.* Earth Pledge Foundation, 2001. An excellent collection of essays covering a wide range of issues in sustainable architectural design.

Edey, Anna. *Solviva: How to Grow $500,000 on One Acre & Peace on Earth.* Trailblazer Press, 1998. A practical guide for implementing greenhouse and alternative food-growing strategies.

Emerson, Ralph Waldo; selected and introduced by Tony Tanner. *Essays and Poems / Ralph Waldo Emerson.* C. E. Tuttle, 1992. A collection depicting the breadth of Emerson's talent.

Fodor, Eben. *Better Not Bigger: How To Take Control of Urban Growth and Improve Your Community.* New Society Publishers, 1999. A helpful guide for communities to use to assess and tackle urban growth issues.

Frankel, Carl. *Out of the Labyrinth: Who We Are, How We Go Wrong and What We Can Do About It.* Monkfish Book Publishing Company, 2004. Presents a framework for understanding ourselves, our culture and ways of working toward a sustainable future.

Giarini, Orio and Walter R. Stahel. *The Limits to Certainty: Facing Risks in the New Service Economy.* 2nd rev. ed., Kluwer Academic Publishers, International Studies in the Service Economy, vol. 4, 1993. An insightful examination of the links between the service economy and the concept of "cradle to cradle" sustainability.

Gladwell, Malcolm. *The Tipping Point: How Little Things Can Make a Big Difference.* Back Bay Books, 2002. An analysis of the genesis and evolution of social transformations.

Goldsmith, Edward. *The Way: An Ecological World View.* Rev. ed., University of Georgia Press, 1998. A compelling case for an alternative ecological and economic model for society.

Goldsmith, Edward, Martin Khor, Helena Norberg-Hodge and Vandana Shiva. *The Future of Progress: Reflections on Environment and Development.* International Society for Ecology and Culture,

1992. Observations and examples for implementing alternative development strategies.

Goldsmith, Edward and Jerry Mander, eds. *The Case Against the Global Economy: And For a Turn Toward the Local.* Kogan Page, 2001. An in-depth analysis of the impact of the global economy from a group of scholars, economists and activists.

Goodall, Jane. *Reason for Hope: A Spiritual Journey.* Warner Books, 1999. An autobiographical account of the noted animal behaviorist's experiences and her optimistic view of the future.

Gottfried, David. *Greed To Green.* Worldbuild Technologies, 2004. The story of a personal journey that revolutionized the building industry through the creation of the US and World Green Building Councils.

Hawken, Paul. *Growing a Business.* Simon and Schuster, 1987. A successful guide for business entrepreneurs, this book spawned the popular television series.

Hawken, Paul. *The Ecology of Commerce: A Declaration of Sustainability.* HarperCollins, 1993. An important work that synthesizes a collection of ideas on sustainable corporate practices.

Hawken, Paul, Amory Lovins and L. Hunter Lovins. *Natural Capitalism: Creating the Next Industrial Revolution.* Little, Brown and Company, 1999. A portrait by three innovative visionaries of the changes occurring as we move into a new industrial revolution.

Heinberg, Richard W. *A New Covenant With Nature: Notes on the End of Civilization and the Renewal of Culture.* Quest Books, 1996. A refreshing perspective on the relationship of society and nature and on the roles of government and the individual.

Heinberg, Richard W. *Cloning the Buddha: The Moral Impact of Biotechnology.* Quest Books, 1999. A well-rounded review of the ethical questions surrounding biotechnology.

Heinberg, Richard W. *The Party's Over: Oil, War and the Fate of Industrial Societies.* New Society Publishers, 2003. Traces the impact of oil on the rise of modern culture and the options we will face when oil inevitably runs out.

Heinberg, Richard W. *Powerdown: Options and Actions for a Post-Carbon World*. New Society Publishers, 2004. Building on his previous work, *The Party's Over: Oil, War and the Fate of Industrial Societies*, this book explores the options for dealing with the world's rising population and dwindling oil reserves.

Hemenway, Toby and John Todd. *Gaia's Garden: A Guide to Home-Scale Permaculture*. Chelsea Green Publishing Company, 2001. A practical look at the conceptual framework and implementation strategies of permaculture design.

Henderson, Hazel. *Paradigms in Progress: Life Beyond Economics*. Knowledge Systems, 1991. Stretching the possibilities of economic thinking by incorporating an integrated approach to measuring progress.

Hertsgaard, Mark. *Earth Odyssey: Around the World in Search of Our Environmental Future*. Broadway Books, 1999. A well-documented and engaging account of the global environmental condition.

Hill, Julia Butterfly. *One Makes the Difference: Inspiring Actions That Change Our World*. HarperSanFrancisco, 2002. An encouraging collection of stories from environmental activists and ideas for individuals interested in creating a sustainable future.

Hock, Dee W. *Birth of the Chaordic Age*. Berrett-Koehler Publishers, 1999. A powerful perspective on alternative organizational models from the architect of the VISA electronic payment system.

Holland, Gail Bernice. *A Call for Connection: Solutions for Creating a Whole New Culture*. New World Library, 1998. An inspiring account of positive change and cultural transformation.

Holmgren, David. *Permaculture: Principles and Pathways Beyond Sustainability*. Holmgren Design Services, 2002. An excellent distillation of the permaculture design principles and their wide range of applications.

International Forum on Globalization. *Alternatives to Economic Globalization: A Better World Is Possible*. 2nd ed., Berrett-Koehler Publishers, 2004. A comprehensive argument against globalization and for an alternative economic model.

Jackson, Wes. *Becoming Native to This Place*. Counterpoint Press,

1996. Explores the significance of place in our relationship to the natural world.

James, Sarah and Torbjörn Lahti. *The Natural Step for Communities: How Cities and Towns can Change to Sustainable Practices.* New Society Publishers, 2004. Inspiring examples of success stories for developing sustainable communities.

Johnson, Huey D. *Green Plans: Greenprint for Sustainability.* University of Nebraska Press, 1995. A thorough examination of the significance of green plans with useful examples from around the world.

Johnston, David R. *Building Green in a Black and White World: A Guide to Selling the Homes Your Customers Want.* Home Builder Press, 2000. A practical look at green building with useful tips for the homebuyer and builder.

Johnston, David R. and Kim Master. *Green Remodeling: Changing the World One Room at a Time.* New Society Publishers, 2004. A comprehensive and practical guide to remodeling your home in a healthful and environmentally friendly way.

Kennedy, Joseph F., ed. *The Art of Natural Building.* New Society Publishers, 2002. A useful collection of general and practical information about natural building geared for both the novice and the professional.

Kilkus, Peter. "Conspiracy Theory or Automatic Pilot: The Economic Roots of Environmental Destruction." N.p., 1999. An in-depth examination of the impact of global financial markets on environmental and social problems.

Kimbrell, Andrew, ed. *Fatal Harvest: The Tragedy of Industrial Agriculture.* Foundation for Deep Ecology, 2002. Describes the devastating impacts of the industrial agricultural system and presents the benefits of an organic and ecological approach to food production.

Leopold, Aldo. *A Sand County Almanac.* 1949. Ballantine Books, Oxford University Press, 1966. The classic work by the renowned American ecologist depicting his views on conservation and the need for an environmental ethic.

Lovins, Amory B., E. Kyle Datta, Odd-Even Bustnes, Jonathan G. Koomey and Nathan J. Glasgow. *Winning the Oil Endgame: Innovation for Profits, Jobs, and Security*. Rocky Mountain Institute, 2004. Presents a comprehensive plan for eliminating US dependence on oil through innovative technologies and smart business strategies.

Macy, Joanna and Molly Young Brown. *Coming Back to Life*. New Society Publishers, 1998. Provides a sound conceptual framework for our current social transformation and practical tools for dealing with the emotional and cultural impact of change.

McDonough, William. *The Hannover Principles: Design for Sustainability*. William McDonough Architects, 1992. Provides the background and conceptual framework for the Hannover Principles.

McDonough, William and Michael Braungart. *Cradle to Cradle: Remaking the Way We Make Things*. North Point Press, 2002. A visionary approach based on using natural systems for rethinking how we design and manufacture products.

McKibben, Bill. *Hope, Human and Wild*. Hungry Mind Press, 1995. An excellent account of positive sustainability trends with examples from upstate New York; Curitiba, Brazil; and Kerala, India.

Meadows, Donella, Jorgen Randers and Dennis L. Meadows. *Limits to Growth: The 30-Year Update*. Chelsea Green Publishing Company, 2004. This updated edition of the classic work presents a sobering look at the limits of the Earth's life-support systems.

Merchant, Carolyn, ed. *Ecology: Key Concepts in Critical Theory*. Humanities Press International, 1994. An anthology of essays on ecological topics including critical theory, economics, social justice and postmodern science.

Minnesota Planning Environmental Quality Board. *Investing in Minnesota's Future: An Agenda for Sustaining Our Quality of Life*. Minnesota Planning, 1998. An excellent example of a statewide sustainability framework, adopted by Minnesota.

Minnesota Planning Environmental Quality Board. *Minnesota Milestones*. Minnesota Planning, 1998. A description of the goals used to evaluate the progress of Minnesota's green plan. For the

2002 update, see <www.mnplan.state.mn.us/mm>.

Mollison, Bill. *Permaculture: A Practical Guide for a Sustainable Future*. Island Press, 1990. One of the essential resources on permaculture, with in-depth coverage of key topics.

Muir, John. *John Muir: Nature Writings: The Story of My Boyhood and Youth; My First Summer in the Sierra; The Mountains of California; Stickeen; Essays*. Library of America, 1997. A comprehensive collection of nature writings by one of America's most renowned wilderness writers.

Naess, Arne, author; Harold Glasser, editor. *The Selected Works of Arne Naess*. Springer, 2005 (forthcoming). A ten-volume set compiling a substantial body of work from one of Norway's most prominent philosophers, the founder of the deep ecology movement.

Nattrass, Brian and Mary Altomare. *The Natural Step for Business: Wealth, Ecology and the Evolutionary Corporation*. New Society Publishers, 1999. Explores the philosophy and implementation of The Natural Step in the business community.

Norberg-Hodge, Helena. *Ancient Futures: Learning from Ladakh*. Sierra Club Books, 1991. The remarkable chronicle of the impact of Western development on the traditional culture of Ladakh in northern India.

Orr, David W. *Ecological Literacy: Education and the Transition to a Postmodern World*. State University of New York, 1992. An argument for integrating ecological concepts into education frameworks.

Orr, David W. *Earth in Mind: On Education, Environment, and the Human Prospect*. Island Press, 1994. A groundbreaking work discussing the role of education from an ecological perspective.

Orr, David W. *The Nature of Design: Ecology, Culture, and Human Intention*. Oxford University Press, 2002. A stimulating appraisal of the possibilities of ecological design for reshaping society.

Orr, David W. *The Last Refuge: Patriotism, Politics, and the Environment in an Age of Terror*. Island Press, 2004. A candid assessment of the shortcomings of the political system and current environmental policies and the opportunities for citizens to actively engage in creating a sustainable future.

Ponting, Clive. *A Green History of the World: The Environment and the Collapse of Great Civilizations*. Penguin Books, 1991. A fascinating historical perspective on the rise and fall of civilizations viewed through an environmental lens.

Ray, Paul H. and Sherry Ruth Anderson *The Cultural Creatives: How 50 Million People Are Changing the World*. Harmony Books, 2000. This work describes the characteristics of an emerging social transformation driven by Cultural Creatives.

Rifkin, Jeremy. *The Hydrogen Economy: The Creation of the Worldwide Energy Web and the Redistribution of Power on Earth*. Jeremy P. Tarcher, 2003. A historical account of the rise of the oil and fossil fuel economy and the transition to hydrogen.

Ryan, John C. and Alan Thein Durning. *Stuff: The Secret Lives of Everyday Things*. Northwest Environment Watch, 1997. The story of the life cycles in our industrial society of items such as newspapers, sneakers and a cup of coffee.

Sale, Kirkpatrick. *Dwellers in the Land: The Bioregional Vision*. University of Georgia Press, 2000. A well-rounded exploration of the principles of bioregionalism.

Savory, Allen and Jody Butterfield. *Holistic Management: A New Framework for Decision Making*. Island Press, 1998. An exploration of the Holistic Management Model, a powerful decision-making framework that incorporates economic, social and environmental factors and is used throughout the world.

Schumacher, E. F. *Small is Beautiful: Economics as if People Mattered*. Harper & Row Publishers, 1973. A portrait of sustainable alternatives by one of the leading visionaries of our time.

Senge, Peter M. *The Fifth Discipline: The Art & Practice of The Learning Organization*. Doubleday/Currency, 1990. An insightful account of applying systems-thinking concepts and other organizational development models in working environments.

Shiva, Vandana. *Monocultures of the Mind: Perspectives on Biodiversity and Biotechnology*. Zed Books, 1993. Outlines the dangers of the loss of biodiversity.

Shiva, Vandana. *Stolen Harvest: The Hijacking of the Global Food*

Supply. South End Press, 1999. Points to the impact of industrial agriculture, genetic engineering and globalization on small farmers, local economies and the quality of food.

Speth, James Gustave. *Red Sky at Morning: America and the Crisis of the Global Environment*. Yale University Press, 2004. A comprehensive review of past environmental efforts and an assessment of strategies for dealing with future environmental challenges.

Sustainable Seattle. *Indicators of Sustainable Community, 1998: A Status Report on Long-Term Cultural, Economic, and Environmental Health for Seattle/King County*. Sustainable Seattle, 1998. One of the pioneer groups that created a national model for developing indicators.

Thoreau, Henry David. *Walden*. 1854. AMS Press, 1982. The classic account of our relationship with nature by one of America's foremost transcendentalist writers.

Todd, John and Nancy Jack Todd. *From Eco-Cities to Living Machines: Principles of Ecological Design*. North Atlantic Books, 1994. A wide selection of sustainable living concepts including innovative agricultural and water purification strategies for urban settings.

Van der Ryn, Sim. *Design for Life: The Architecture of Sim Van der Ryn*. Gibbs Smith Publishers, 2005. Describes the author's ecological design principles and strategies and his architectural work.

Van der Ryn, Sim and Peter Calthorpe. *Sustainable Communities*. Random House, 1991. Innovative approaches to designing and implementing sustainable communities.

Van der Ryn, Sim and Stuart Cowan. *Ecological Design*. Island Press, 1995. Explores a range of ecological principles and their implementation in architectural design.

Waage, Sissel. *Ants, Galileo, and Gandhi: Designing the Future of Business through Nature, Genius, and Compassion*. Renouf Publishing Company, 2003. A systems perspective on creating and implementing a sustainability framework for business and industry, this work is based on scientific principles and backed by compelling case studies.

Wackernagel, Mathis and William Rees. *Our Ecological Footprint: Reducing Human Impact on the Earth*. New Society Publishers, 1996. The description of an innovative tool for assessing human impact.

Weisman, Alan. *Gaviotas: A Village to Reinvent the World*. Chelsea Green Publishing Company, 1995. The inspiring success story of an ecovillage established in the seemingly inhospitable Colombian countryside.

Wheatley, Margaret J. *Leadership and the New Science: Discovering Order in a Chaotic World*. Rev. ed., Berrett-Koehler Publishers, 2001. An innovative approach presenting a framework that bridges natural systems and organizational development.

Wheatley, Margaret J. *Turning to One Another: Simple Conversations to Restore Hope to the Future*. Berrett-Koehler Publishers, 2002. Highlights the value of conversation as a catalyst in the process of discovering solutions and creating change.

Wilson, Edward O. *The Diversity of Life*. Belknap Press, Harvard University, 1992. An engaging view of the marvels of biodiversity and the effects of human activities.

Wilson, Edward O. *Consilience: The Unity of Knowledge*. Vintage Books, 1998. An intriguing perspective on knowledge and how disciplines are linked by a set of natural laws.

Wise, John C. "A Journey Towards Sustainability." N.p., 1999. A thorough review of the concepts of sustainability including values, obstacles and trends. See also <www.azalliance.org/Sustainability/svsdev1.pdf>.

World Commission on Environment and Development. *Our Common Future*. Oxford University Press, 1987. A landmark publication on sustainability in the international arena.

Worldwatch Institute. *Vital Signs 2003: The Trends That Are Shaping Our Future*. W.W. Norton and Company, 2003. An annual publication started in 1992 listing global ecological, economic and social indicators.

Worldwatch Institute. *State of the World 2005*. W.W. Norton and Company, 2005. An annual publication started in the 1980s describing sustainability issues and global trends.

NOTES

Introduction

1. For more information, see: Earth Island Institute. *The Borneo Project* [online]. [Cited December 30, 2004]. <www.earthisland.org/borneo>
2. Seth Zukerman. *Concepts in Action: The Redemption of the Astoria Mill Site* [online]. [Cited August 30, 2004]. Ecotrust. <www.ecotrust.org/community/astoria_mill.html>
3. *"Germany shines a beam on the future of energy." The San Francisco Chronicle.* December 20, 2004, p. A1. See also SFGate.com [online]. [Cited December 20, 2004]. <www.sfgate.com>
4. *Efficient Transportation for Successful Urban Planning in Curitiba* [online]. [Cited July 14, 2004]. Horizon: Solutions Site. <www.solutions-site.org/artman/publish/printer_62.shtml>
5. Worldwatch Institute. *State of the World 2004.* W.W. Norton and Company, 2004, p. 3.
6. Lester R. Brown. *Eco-Economy: Building an Economy for the Earth.* W. W. Norton and Company, 2001, pp. 17-18.
7. The World Commission on Environment and Development. *Our Common Future.* Oxford University Press, 1987, p. 43.
8. Renewables for Sustainable Village Power. *National Biogas Dissemination Program* [online]. [Cited August 30, 2004]. <www.rsvp.nrel.gov/asp/project.asp?ID=240#BASIC>
9. Grameen Bank [online]. [Cited July 12, 2004]. <www.grameen-info.org>
10. David Korten. "Corporate Futures." *YES! Magazine.* Summer 1999 [online].[Cited December 2, 2004]. <www.futurenet.org/ article.asp?ID=752>
11. Paul H. Ray and Sherry Ruth Anderson. *The Cultural Creatives: How 50 Million People Are Changing the World.* Harmony Books, 2000, pp. 4, 329. See also [online]. [Cited December 30, 2004]. <www.culturalcreatives.org>
12. Paul Hawken. "The Resurgence of Citizens' Movements." *Earth Light.* Issue 40, vol. 11, no. 3, Winter 2001, p. 10.
13. For details on The Natural Step, see Chapter 2: "Sustainability and Commerce."
14. World Social Forum [online]. [Cited July 27, 2004]. <www.wsfindia.org/anotherworld.php>

15. Carolyn Merchant. *Ecological Revolutions: Nature, Gender, and Science in New England.* University of North Carolina Press, 1989, p. 270.

Chapter 1

1. Ralph Waldo Emerson. "The Transcendentalist: A Lecture read at the Masonic Temple, Boston, January, 1842." *Dial: A Magazine for Literature, Philosophy, and Religion.* Vol. 3 (1842-43), p. 297.
2. For background information on Emerson's writings, including *Nature*, see Transcendentalists. *Ralph Waldo Emerson* [online]. [Cited January 20, 2005].
   <www.transcendentalists.com/1emerson.html>
3. The Walden Woods Project. *Walden: Where I Lived and What I Lived For* [online]. [Cited December 22, 2004].
   <www.walden.org/Institute/thoreau/writings/walden/02_whereilived.htm>
4. John Muir. *The Yosemite.* The Century Co., 1912, p. 256.
5. John Muir Exhibit. *John Muir: A Brief Biography* [online]. [Cited September 23, 2004]. <www.sierraclub.org/john_muir_exhibit/life/muir_biography.html>
6. Aldo Leopold. *A Sand County Almanac.* 1949. Ballantine Books, Oxford University Press, 1966, p. 239.
7. See, for example, William K. Stevens. "Celebrating an Ecologist's Eloquence and Vision." *The New York Times.* October 19, 1999, p. D4.
8. International Institute of Sustainable Development. *Sustainable Development Timeline* [online]. [Cited September 23, 2004].
   <http://iisd.ca/rio+5/timeline/sdtimeline.htm>
9. US Environmental Protection Agency. *Superfund 20th Anniversary Report* [online]. [Cited December 12, 2004]. Chapter 1: "Continuing the Promise of Earth Day."
   <www.epa.gov/superfund/action/20years/ch1pg1.htm>
10. United Nations. *United Nations Conference on the Human Environment (Stockholm, 1972)* [online]. [Cited August 30, 2004]. United Nations Conferences: Selected Materials Available in the Michigan State University Libraries and on the WWW.
    <www.lib.msu.edu/publ_ser/docs/igos/unconfs.htm#humen>
11. United Nations Environment Programme (UNEP). *The Organization, Mission Statement* [online]. [Cited September 23, 2004].
    <www.unep.org/Documents/Default.asp?DocumentID=43>
12. University of Washington Superfund Basic Research Program. *The History of Superfund* [online]. [Cited December 2, 2004].
    <http://depts.washington.edu/sfund/history.html> See also US Environmental Protection Agency. *Superfund 20th Anniversary Report* [online]. [Cited December 2, 2004].
    <www.epa.gov/ superfund/action/20years>.

13. The World Commission on Environment and Development. *Our Common Future.* Oxford University Press, 1987, p. ix.
14. International Institute of Sustainable Development. *Sustainable Development Timeline* [online]. [Cited September 23, 2004]. <http://iisd.ca/rio+5/timeline/sdtimeline.htm>
15. The World Commission on Environment and Development. *Our Common Future.* Oxford University Press, 1987,. p. 43.
16. Ibid., p. 5.
17. Ibid., p. 8.
18. Ibid., p. 49.
19. Global Tomorrow Coalition. *Sustainable Development Tool Kit* [online]. [Cited June 7, 2000]. <www.iisd.org/educate/learn/agenda21.doc>
20. United Nations Association in Canada. *The UN and Sustainable Development: History* [online]. [Cited November 24, 1999]. <www.unac.org/monitor/SusDev/background/what_is_SusDev.html>
21. President's Council on Sustainable Development. *Overview* [online]. [Cited December 30, 2004]. <http://clinton2.nara.gov/PCSD/ Overview> For further information, see President's Council on Sustainable Development [online]. [Cited January 22, 2005]. <http://clinton2.nara.gov/PCSD>
22. President's Council on Sustainable Development. *Final Report* [online]. [Cited December 30, 2004]. Press release, May 5, 1999. <http://clinton2.nara.gov/PCSD/pressrep.html> For further information see President's Council on Sustainable Development [online]. [Cited January 22, 2005]. <http://clinton2.nara.gov/PCSD>
23. International Institute for Sustainable Development. *Earth Negotiations Bulletin* [online]. [Cited July 14, 2004]. Vol. 22, no. 51 (September 6, 2002), p 1. <www.iisd.ca/linkages/2002/wssd/>
24. Ibid., p.17.
25. Gretchen C. Daily, ed. *Nature's Services: Societal Dependence on Natural Ecosystems.* Island Press, 1997. Pp. 3-4.
26. Paul Hawken, Amory Lovins and L. Hunter Lovins. *Natural Capitalism.* Little, Brown & Co., 1999, pp. 3-5. See Natural Capitalism [online]. [Cited June 7, 2000]. <www.natcap.org>
27. I am indebted in this section to the work of Margaret Pennington of Sustainable Sonoma, Santa Rosa, California.
28. I am indebted to John C. Wise for his contribution to the understanding of the role of education in the Three Es. For further information, see: John C. Wise. "A Journey Towards Sustainability." N.p. 1999.
29. *Webster's College Dictionary.* Random House, 1991.
30. I am indebted to David Caploe for his suggestions on organizing this

section. For a full discussion of the methodological assumptions behind this section, see his forthcoming book, *Shadows On A Cave Wall*, Chapter 4: "Max Weber and a Democratic Theory of Objectivity."

31. For further review of the role of sustainability in higher education, see Second Nature: Education for Sustainability [online]. [Cited September 3, 2004]. <www.secondnature.org>

32. Bruce Chatwin. *The Songlines*. Viking Penguin, 1987, p. 13.

Chapter 2

1. For further details on Progress Indicators, see: Minnesota Planning. *Smart Signals: An Assessment of Progress Indicators* [online]. [Cited July 27, 2004]. Minnesota Department of Administration, 2000. <http://server.admin.state.mn.us/resource. html?Id=1963>

2. College of Law, National Taiwan University. *Sustainable Communities Resource Package: Sustainable Communities 2.3. A Vision of Community Sustainability: Model Principles* [online]. [Cited December 10, 2004]. <www.law.ntu.edu.tw/sustain/ intro/ortee/20/23vision.html>

3. Minnesota Planning Environmental Quality Board. *Investing in Minnesota's Future: An Agenda for Sustaining Our Quality of Life*. Minnesota Planning,1998. Editor's Page. See also [online]. [Cited December 30, 2004]. <www.mnplan.state.mn.us/ pdf/1999/eqb/vision.pdf>

4. Ibid.

5. Ibid., p.3.

6. Additional states considering statewide sustainable development plans include Maryland, New Jersey, Oregon and Pennsylvania. For a regional approach to principles of sustainability (in the US Great Plains) see: International Institute for Sustainable Development. *The Principles for Great Plains Sustainability* [online]. [September 24, 2004]. <http://iisd1.iisd.ca/agri/ gpprinciples.htm>

7. For additional information about The Bellagio Principles for Assessment, see: National Strategies for Sustainable Development [online]. [Cited December 3, 2004]. <www.nssd.net/references/ SDInd/Bellagio.html>

8. For additional information about Sustainable Seattle, see: Sustainable Seattle [online]. [Cited September 3, 2004]. <www.sustainableseattle.org>

9. For a summary of the progress of sustainability plans for Minnesota, New Jersey and Oregon see: Resource Renewal Institute. *RRI Archives USA* [online]. [Cited July 27, 2004]. <http://greenplans.rri.org/resources/greenplanningarchives/usa/archives_usa.html>

10. For additional information on New Jersey's green plan, see: New Jersey Sustainable State Institute [online]. [Cited December 30, 2004].

<http://njssi.net>; New Jersey Future [online]. [Cited December 30, 2004]. <www.njfuture.org>; and *Governing with the Future in Mind* [online]. [Cited December 30, 2004]. <www.state.nj.us/dep/dsr/governing> For information on Oregon's green plan, see Oregon Solutions [online]. [Cited July 27, 2004]. <www.sustainableoregon.net>

11. Patricia Scruggs. *A Summary of the Dutch NEPP (National Environmental Policy Plan)* [online]. [Cited July 27, 2004]. Resource Renewal Institute, 1993.
    <http://greenplans.rri.org/resources/greenplanningarchives/netherlands/netherlands_1993_ nepp.html>

12. Resource Renewal Institute. *Snapshot of the Development of NEPP4* [online]. [Cited July 27, 2004].
    <http://greenplans.rri.org/resources/greenplanningarchives/netherlands/netherlands_nepp4.html>

13. For a summary of NEPP4, see: Resource Renewal Institute. *Update on National Environmental Policy Plan 4 (NEPP4), January 2000* [online]. [Cited July 27, 2004].
    <http://greenplans.rri.org/resources/greenplanningarchives/netherlands/netherlands_nepp4.html>

14. Resource Renewal Institute. *The Netherlands Environmental Policy Profile: Guiding Principles* [online]. [Cited July 27, 2004].
    <http://greenplans.rri.org/resources/greenplanningarchives/netherlands/netherlands_1995epp_guidpr.html#principles>

15. For further discussion of the precautionary principle, see Chapter 3: "Sustainability and Commerce."

16. For further information and to calculate your own ecological footprint, see: Ecological Footprint Network [online]. [Cited July 27, 2004]. <www.footprintnetwork.net> See also Mathis Wackernagel and William Rees in the Annotated Bibliography.

17 Global Footprint Network. *About the Ecological Footprint* [online]. [Cited September 3, 2004]. <www.footprintnetwork.net>

18. Global Footprint Network. *The Ecological Footprint: Examples of Existing Applications* [online]. [Cited September 3, 2004]. <www.footprintnetwork.net> See also: Sustainable Sonoma County. *The Ecological Footprint Project* [online]. [Cited September 3, 2004]. <www.sustainablesonoma.org/projects/scefootprint.html>

19. Resource Renewal Institute. *The Netherlands Environmental Policy Profile: Guiding Principles* [online]. [Cited July 27, 2004].
    <http://greenplans.rri.org/resources/greenplanningarchives/netherlands/netherlands_1995epp_guidpr.html#principles>

20. Resource Renewal Institute. *Update on National Environmental Policy Plan 4 (NEPP4), January 2000* [online]. [Cited July 27, 2004].
    <http://greenplans.rri.org/resources/greenplanningarchives/netherlands/netherlands_nepp4.html>

21. The Earth Charter Initiative. *Introduction* [online]. [Cited July 27, 2004]. <www.earthcharter.org>

22. This is an abbreviated version. For the complete Earth Charter, see: The Earth Charter Initiative [online]. [Cited July 27, 2004]. <www.earthcharter.org/files/charter/charter.pdf>

23. The Earth Charter Initiative. *Earth Charter and Local Communities* [online]. [Cited July 27, 2004]. <www.earthcharter.org/innerpg.cfm?id_menu=25>

24. ICLEI - Local Governments for Sustainability. *About ICLEI* [online]. [Cited July 28, 2004]. <www.iclei.org/about.htm>

25. International Institute for Sustainable Development. *Briefcase for the World Summit on Sustainable Development: Small is Bountiful* [online]. [Cited July 28, 2004]. <www.iisd.org/briefcase/ten+ten_success2.asp>

26. ICLEI — Local Governments for Sustainability. *Cities for Climate Protection* [online]. [Cited July 28, 2004]. <www.iclei.org/ co2/index.htm>

Chapter 3

1. SustainAbility. *SD Issues: What is the Triple Bottom Line?* [online]. [Cited December 2, 2004]. <www.sustainability. com/philosophy/triple-bottom/tbl-intro.asp>

2. Interface Sustainability. *Global Metrics* [online]. [Cited September 24, 2004]. <www.interfacesustainability.com/ metrics.html> and personal communication.

3. Interface Sustainability. *The Seven Fronts. Redesign Commerce* [online]. [Cited March 29, 2005]. <www.interfacesustainability.com/visi.html>

4. Arup. *SPeAR®: Product overview* [online]. [Cited July 28, 2004]. <www.arup.com/environment/feature.cfm?pageid=1685>

5. For additional information on LCA, see: Life Cycle Assessment Links [online]. [Cited December 8, 2004]. <www.life-cycle.org> and US Environmental Protection Agency. *Life-Cycle Assessment LCAccess* [online]. [Cited December 8, 2004]. <www.epa.gov/ ORD/NRMRL/lcaccess>

6. *Global Sullivan Principles of Social Responsibilty* [online]. [Cited December 21, 2004]. <http://globalsullivanprinciples.org/principles.htm>

7. Global Reporting Initiative. *Addition of New Reporters Results in New Landmark for GRI* [online]. [Cited December 2, 2004]. News, November 24, 2004. <www.globalreporting.org/news/updates/article.asp?ArticleID =364>

8. Global Reporting Initiative. *Vision and Mission Statements* [online].

[Cited July 28, 2004].
<www.globalreporting.org/ about/mission.asp>

9. In this section, I am indebted to the work of Jean Rogers, Senior Sustainability Consultant, Arup, San Francisco, California.

10. For additional information see: The Equator Principles [online]. [Cited July 28, 2004]. <www.equator-principles.com>

11. The Equator Principles. *Putting Principles into Practice* [online]. [Cited July 28, 2004].
<www.equator-principles.com/ ef2.shtml>

12. For further information on the precautionary principle, see: Ag Biotech InfoNet. *Precautionary Principle* [online]. [Cited August 30, 2004]. <www.biotech-info.net/precautionary.html> and The Lowell Center for Sustainable Production. *International Summit on Science and the Precautionary Principle* [online]. [Cited August 30, 2004]. <http://sustainableproduction.org/ precaution>

13. The New Canadian Environmental Protection Act (CEPA). *The Precautionary Principle/Approach: History, Scope and Spectrums of Meaning* [online]. [Cited April 27, 2000].
<www.ec.gc.ca/ cepa/ip18/e18_01.html#J00>

14. Rachel's Environment & Health Weekly. *The Precautionary Principle* [online]. [Cited December 3, 2004]. No. 586, February 19, 1998.
<www.monitor.net/rachel/r586.html>

15. Ibid.

16. For further details on genetically modified salmon, see: "Altered Salmon Leading Way To Dinner Plates, but Rules Lag." *The New York Times.* May 1, 2000, p. 1.

17. The Baltic Marine Environment Protection Commission. *The Helsinki Convention: Convention on the Protection of the Marine Environment of the Baltic Sea Area, 1992 (entered into force on 17 January 2000)* [online]. [Cited August 30, 2004].
<www.helcom.fi/helcom/convention.html>

18. United Nations Framework Convention on Climate Change [online]. [Cited December 3, 2004].
<http://unfccc.int/ 2860.php>

19. For more information, see: Convention on Biological Diversity. Cartagena Protocol on Biosafety [online]. [Cited August 30, 2004]. <www.biodiv.org/biosafety/protocol.asp>

20. San Francisco Department of the Environment. *San Francisco Precautionary Principle Ordinance* [online]. [Cited September 7, 2004]. <http://temp.sfgov.org/sfenvironment/aboutus/policy/ legislation/precaution_principle.htm>

21. The Natural Step's Four System Conditions can be seen at Oregon Natural Step [online]. [Cited December 30, 2004].
<www.ortns.org/faq.asp> For additional information, see The Natural

Step Canada [online]. [Cited March 16, 2005]. <www.naturalstep.ca/framework.html>

22. For more information on the science of The Natural Step, see: The Natural Step Canada *Basic Science* [online]. [Cited March 16, 2005]. <www.naturalstep.ca/basicscience.html>

23. Ibid.

24. For more details on ecosystem services, see: Gretchen C. Daily, ed. *Nature's Services: Societal Dependence on Natural Ecosystems.* Island Press, 1997.

25. For further details, see: The Oregon Natural Step. *Case Studies* [online]. [Cited March 16, 2005]. <www.ortns.org/resources.asp>

26. The Natural Step Canada *The Funnel* [online]. [Cited March 16, 2005]. <www.naturalstep.ca/the funnel.html>

27. The Alliance for Sustainable Jobs and the Environment. Houston Principles of the Alliance for Sustainable Jobs and the Environment [online]. [Cited August 30, 2004]. <www.asje.org/houston.html>

28. Ibid.

29. Coalition for Environmentally Responsible Economies (CERES). *About Us* [online]. [Cited January 21, 2005]. <www.ceres.org/about/main.htm>

30. Coalition for Environmentally Responsible Economies (CERES). *Our Work: The CERES Principles* [online]. [Cited August 30, 2004]. <www.ceres.org/our_work/principles.htm>

31. International Chamber of Commerce. *Introducing the International Chamber of Commerce* [online]. [Cited August 30, 2004]. <www.iccwbo.org/home/intro_icc/introducing_icc.asp>

32. International Organization for Standardization. *Environmental Management. The ISO 14000 Family of International Standards* [online]. [Cited August 30, 2004]. <www.iso.ch/9000e/meet/ 14k.htm>

33. Brian Dunkiel, M. Jeff Hammond and Jim Motavalli. "Sharing the Wealth: If We Shift the Tax Burden From Work to Waste, Everyone Benefits." *E-Magazine.* Vol. X, no. 2 (March/April 1999), p. 34.

34. Alan Thein Durning and Yoram Bauman. *Tax Shift.* Northwest Environment Watch, 1998, pp. 6-7.

Chapter 4

1. American Petroleum Institute. *About API: Mission.* [online]. [Cited September 1, 2004]. <http://api-ec.api.org/aboutapi>

2. American Petroleum Institute. *Environmental Commitment: API's Environmental, Health and Safety Mission and Guiding Principles* [online]. [Cited December 21, 2004].

<http://api-ec.api.org>

3. For additional information on forest certification systems, see: Forest Certification Resource Center [online]. [Cited December 8, 2004]. <www.certifiedwood.org>

4. Forest Stewardship Council. *About FSC* [online]. [Cited July 29, 2004]. <www.fsc.org/fsc/about>

5. See Chapter 3: "Sustainability and Commerce" for discussion of the Houston Principles and Maxxam Corporation's role in logging redwood trees in Northern California.

6. For a complete description of FSC Principles and Criteria, see Forest Stewardship Council. *Policy & Standards: FSC Principles & Criteria of Forest Stewardship* [online]. [Cited July 29, 2004]. <www.fsc.org/fsc/how_fsc_works/policy_standards/princ_criteria>

7. James Gustave Speth. *Red Sky at Morning: America and the Crisis of the Global Environment.* Yale University Press, 2004, pp. 89-90.

8. Rainforest Action Network. *Old Growth Campaign: Boise Victory* [online]. [Cited July 29, 2004]. <www.ran.org/ran_campaigns/old_growth/victory.html> See also: Boise Environment. *Boise and the Environment Report 2003* [online]. [Cited July 29, 2004]. <http://boise.bc.com/environment>

9. Marine Stewardship Council. *Fisheries: Principles and Criteria for Sustainable Fishing* [online]. [Cited August 6, 2004]. <www.msc.org/html/content_463.htm>

10. Worldwatch Institute. *State of the World 2000.* W.W. Norton and Company, 2000, p. 188.

11. Ibid., p. 8.

12. Marine Stewardship Council. *About MSC: Mission, Vision, Values* [online]. [Cited August 6, 2004]. <www.msc.org/html/ content_482.htm>

13. For review of the FAO's Code of Conduct for Responsible Fisheries, see: [online]. [Cited December 30, 2004]. <www.fao.org/fi/agreem/codecond/codecon.asp>

14. Marine Stewardship Council. *Go Wild With Alaskan Salmon* [online]. [Cited August 6, 2004]. Press release, January 9, 2004. <www.msc.org/html/ni_105.htm>

15. For the complete Principles and Criteria document, see Marine Stewardship Council. *MSC Standard — Ps and Cs* [online]. [Cited September 24, 2004]. <www.msc.org/html/content_504.htm>

16. Worldwatch Institute. *State of the World 2000.* W.W. Norton and Company, 2000, pp.187-188.

17. Worldwatch Institute. *State of the World 2004.* W.W. Norton and Company, 2004, p. 70.

18. Worldwatch Institute. *State of the World 2000*. W.W. Norton and Company, 2000, pp.189-191.
19. For a complete description of the MSC Principles, see [online]. [Cited September 24, 2004]. <www.msc.org.html/content_ 504.htm> For further discussion of the precautionary principle, see Chapter 3: "Sustainability and Commerce."
20. Alliance for Sustainability. *Background on the International Alliance for Sustainable Agriculture* [online]. [Cited August 31, 2004]. <www.mtn.org/iasa/bckgrnd.htm>
21. Alliance for Sustainability. *Seven Challenges* [online]. [Cited August 31, 2004]. <www.mtn.org/iasa/asilo.htm>
22. Protected Harvest. *About Us* [online]. [Cited August 11, 2004]. <www.protectedharvest.org/aboutus/mission.htm>
23. Protected Harvest. *The Standards* [online]. [Cited December 30, 2004]. <www.protectedharvest.org/farmers/standards.htm>
24. Wine Institute. *Sustainable Winegrowing Practices Project Description* [online]. [Cited August 13, 2004]. <www.wineinstitute.org/communications/SustainablePractices/project_description.htm>.
25. California Association of Winegrape Growers. *Workbook: Introductory Chapter* [online]. [Cited August 13, 2004]. <www.cawg.org/pdf/sustainability-wkbk_1.pdf >

Chapter 5

1. U.S. Green Building Council. *An Introduction to the U.S. Green Building Council and the LEED Green Building Rating System* [online]. [Cited December 22, 2004]. <www.usgbc.org/ Resources/research.asp>
2. The Product-Life Institute, Geneva [online]. [Cited December 20, 2004]. <www.product-life.org>
3. William McDonough. *The Hannover Principles: Design for Sustainability*. William McDonough Architects, 1992. Author's Note.
4. Ibid., pp. 8-9. See also: [online]. [Cited December 22, 2004]. <www.mcdonough.com/principles.pdf>
5. William McDonough and Michael Braungart. *Cradle to Cradle: Remaking the Way We Make Things*. North Point Press, 2002, pp. 100-105.
6. Ibid., pp. 102-117. See also: Cynthia Pollock Shea, ed. *Mimicking Nature by Designing Out Waste* [online]. [Cited December 20, 2004]. Florida Sustainable Communities Center, August 14, 2000. <http://sustainable.state.fl.us/fdi/fscc/news/ world/0008/eco-in.htm>
7. William McDonough. *The Hannover Principles: Design for Sustainability*. William McDonough Architects, 1992, p. 112. See also: [online]. [Cited December 22, 2004].

<www.mcdonough.com/principles.pdf>

8. Sim Van der Ryn and Stuart Cowan. *Ecological Design*. Island Press, 1995. See also: The Ecological Design Institute. *Five Principles of Ecological Design* [online]. [Cited December 30, 2004]. <www.ecodesign.org/edi/ecodesign.html>

9. John and Nancy Jack Todd. *From Eco-Cities to Living Machines: Principles of Ecological Design*. North Atlantic Books, 1994, pp. xiv-xv.

10. Donald Aitken Associates. *Useful Information Resources, Sustainable Cities: The Sanborn Principles for Sustainable Development* [online]. [Cited December 16, 2004]. <www.donaldaitkenassociates. com/sanborn_daa.html> and personal communication.

11. See U.S. Green Building Council [online]. [Cited December 30, 2004]. <www.usgbc.org> for details about the organization and LEED. For USGBC and LEED publications, see: [online]. [Cited December 30, 2004]. <www.usgbc.org/LEED/publications.asp>

12. U.S. Green Building Council. *Meet the USGBC: Mission Statement* [online]. [Cited August 3, 2004]. <www.usgbc.org/AboutUs/mission_facts.asp>

13. US Green Building Council. *An Introduction to the U.S. Green Building Council and the LEED Green Building Rating System* [online]. [Cited December 22, 2004]. <www.usgbc.org/ Resources/research.asp>

14. State of California. Office of the Governor. *Governor on Energy: 'More Power, Lower Prices'* [online]. [Cited December 16, 2004]. Executive Order S-20-04 by the Governor of the State of California, December 11, 2004. <www.governor.ca.gov/state/ govsite/gov_homepage.jsp>

15. U.S. Green Building Council. *An Introduction to the U.S. Green Building Council and LEED Green Building Rating System* [online}. [Cited December 22, 2004]. <www.usgbc.org/ Resources/research.asp>

16. William McDonough and Michael Braungart. *Cradle to Cradle: Remaking the Way We Make Things*. North Point Press, 2002, pp. 76, 78.

17. Ibid., pp. 90-91.

Chapter 6

1. Arne Naess. "The Shallow and the Deep, Long-Range Ecology Movements: A Summary." *Inquiry*.Vol. 16, 1973, pp. 95-100. See also Alamut. *The Shallow and the Deep* [online]. [Cited January 17, 2005]. <www.alamut.com/subj/ideologies/ pessimism/Naess_deepEcology.html>. For further discussion, see: Frank B. Golley. Deep Ecology from the Perspective of Ecological Science

[online]. [Cited January 18, 2005]. University of Minnesota College of Natural Resources. <www.fw.umn.edu/NRES3011/DeepECOL.html>; University of Oslo, Centre for Development and the Environment. *Arne Naess: Ecophilosophy and Ecology* [online]. [Cited January 19, 2005]. <www.sum.uio.no/staff/arnena>; and Arne Naess in the Annotated Bibliography.

2. Bill Devall and George Sessions. *Deep Ecology: Living as if Nature Mattered.* Peregrine Smith Books, Gibbs Smith Publishers, 1985,. p. 70. See also: Foundation for Deep Ecology. *Deep Ecology Platform* [online]. [Cited December 14, 2004]. <www.deepecology.org/deepplatform.html>

3. Gender and Sustainable Development. Charter of Rights for the Environment by Ann Dale, Sustainable Development Research Institute [online]. [Cited December 30, 2004]. <www.royalroads.ca/ste/research/gender/charter.html>

4. Janine M. Benyus. *Biomimicry.* William Morrow and Company, 1997. P. 7. See also: Biomimicry. *Chapter One* [online]. [Cited December 30, 2004]. <www.biomimicry.org/chapter_one.html>

5. Ibid.

6. Bill Mollison. *Permaculture: A Practical Guide for a Sustainable Future.* Island Press, 1990, p. ix.

7. For further discussion on patterns, see: Chapter 4: "Pattern Understanding" in Bill Mollison. *Permaculture: A Practical Guide for a Sustainable Future.* Island Press, 1990, pp. 70-105.

8. For further details, see: Permaculture Credit Union [online]. [Cited September 24, 2004]. <www.pcuonline.org>

9. Bill Mollison. *Permaculture: A Practical Guide for a Sustainable Future.* Island Press, 1990, p. 35. See also: permaculture.biz. Bill Mollison Permaculture Principles [online]. [Cited December 30, 2004]. <www.permaculture.biz/mollison.htm>

10. For further information about the National Park Service's *Guiding Principles of Sustainable Design*, see [online]. [Cited December 30, 2004. <www.nps.gov/dsc/dsgncnstr/gpsd/ toc.html> For the National Ski Areas Association's Environmental Charter, see *Sustainable Slopes* [online]. [Cited December 30, 2004]. <www. nsaa.org/nsaa/environment/sustainable_slopes/charter2k.pdf>

Chapter 7

1. For further information about Gaviotas, see Alan Weisman's *Gaviotas: A Village to Reinvent the World* and for information about Curitiba and Kerala, see Bill McKibben's *Hope, Human and Wild*, both listed in the Annotated Bibliography.

2. *Friends of Gaviotas. About Gaviotas: Reading* [online]. [Cited August 13, 2004]. <www.friendsofgaviotas.org/about.htm>

3. ICLEI. *Orienting Urban Planning to Sustainability in Curitiba, Brazil*

[online]. [Cited December 30, 2004].
<www3.iclei.org/ localstrategies/summary/curitiba2.html>
4. Ibid.
5. Govt. of Kerala. *Kerala at a Glance* [online]. [Cited December 22, 2004].
<www.kerala.gov.in/ataglance/ataglance.htm>
6. Akash Kapur. "Poor But Prosperous." *Atlantic Monthly.* Vol. 282
(September 1998), pp. 40-45. See also [online]. [Cited July 14, 2000].
<www.theatlantic.com/issues/98sep/kerala.htm>
7. Worldwatch Institute. *State of the World 2000.* W.W. Norton and
Company, 2000, p. 5.
8. Ibid., p. 16.
9. Ibid., pp. 16-21.
10. Redefining Progress. *Why Bigger Isn't Better: The Genuine Progress
Indicator: 1999 — Present* [online]. [Cited August 20, 2004].
<www.redefiningprogress.org/publications/gpi1999/gpi1999.html> See
also: Worldwatch Institute. State of the World 2004. W.W Norton and
Company, 2004, pp. 164-179.
11. Resource Renewal Institute. *Snapshot of the Development of NEPP4*
[online]. [Cited September 1, 2004].
<http://greenplans.rri.org/resources/greenplanningarchives/
netherlands/netherlands_nepp4.html>
12. For further information on the use of metaphors in sustainability, see
Susan Strong. *The Metaphor Project Description* [online]. [Cited
September 1, 2004].
<www.co-intelligence.org/metaphorproject_descrp.html>
13. James Gustave Speth. *Red Sky at Morning: America and the Crisis of the
Global Environment.* Yale University Press, 2004, p.189. See also: Norman
Myers et. al. "Biodiversity Hotspots for Conservation Priorities." Nature.
Vol. 403, no. 6772 (February 24, 2000), pp. 853-858.
14. James Gustave Speth. *Red Sky at Morning: America and the Crisis of the
Global Environment.* Yale University Press, 2004, p. 190.
15. Natural Capitalism Solutions. *Our Principles* [online]. [Cited December
21, 2004]. <www.natcapsolutions.org> See also: Paul Hawken, Amory
Lovins and L. Hunter Lovins. *Natural Capitalism: Creating the Next
Industrial Revolution.* Little, Brown and Company, 1999, pp. 10-21; and
Natural Capitalism [online]. [Cited December 21, 2004]. <www.nat-
cap.org>
16. The Savory Center. *About Holistic Management* [online]. [Cited
December 21, 2004]. <www.holisticmanagement.org>
17. Solari. *Who We Are* [online]. [Cited September 22, 2004].
<www.solari.com/about/index.htm>
18. James Gustave Speth. *Red Sky at Morning: America and the Crisis of the
Global Environment.* Yale University Press, 2004, p. 186.
19. Ibid.

20. For further information about the U.N. Global Compact, see: Joseph Kahn. "Multinationals Sign U.N. Pact on Rights and Environment." *The New York Times*. July 27, 2000, Front Page. See also: The Global Compact [online]. [Cited August 20, 2004]. <www.unglobalcompact.org>

21. Dean Murphy. "For Solar Power, Foggy City Maps Its Bright Spots." *The New York Times*. November 24, 2002, section 1, p. 24.

22. For further information about efforts to promote sustainability education in colleges and universities, see: Second Nature: Education for Sustainability [online]. [Cited August 30, 2004]. <www.secondnature.org>

23. For details on the Talloires Declaration, see: Association of University Leaders for a Sustainable Future [online]. [Cited September 3, 2004]. <www.ulsf.org/programs_talloires.html> For further discussion of ecological literacy, refer to David W. Orr in the Annotated Bibliography. Also contact: The Center for Ecoliteracy. [online]. [Cited December 30, 2004. <www.ecoliteracy.org>

INDEX

About the Author

ANDRES R. EDWARDS is an educator, author, media designer and environmental systems consultant. He has served as producer, exhibit developer, and consultant for projects in natural history, biodiversity and sustainable community in Northern California, Florida, Missouri, Alaska, Illinois, Washington D.C., Taejon, Korea and Kerala, India. He is co-author of *Tibet: Enduring Spirit, Exploited Land*, about the traditional livelihood of nomads and farmers on the Tibetan Plateau. He holds a BA degree in Geography from the University of Colorado; an MPS in Media Studies from NYU's Interactive Telecommunications Program and an MA in Humanities and Leadership/Culture, Ecology and Sustainable Community from New College of California, Santa Rosa. Mr. Edwards is founder and president of EduTracks, an exhibit design and fabrication firm specializing in green building and sustainability education programs for parks, towns, and companies. He lives with his wife, Rochelle and three children in Northern California. For further regularly updated information, or to contact the author, please visit www.sustainabilityrevolution.com

If you have enjoyed *The Sustainability Revolution,* you might also enjoy other

BOOKS TO BUILD A NEW SOCIETY

Our books provide positive solutions for people who
want to make a difference. We specialize in:

**Environment and Justice • Conscientious Commerce
Sustainable Living • Ecological Design and Planning
Natural Building & Appropriate Technology • New Forestry
Educational and Parenting Resources • Nonviolence
Progressive Leadership • Resistance and Community**

New Society Publishers

ENVIRONMENTAL BENEFITS STATEMENT

New Society Publishers has chosen to produce this book on recycled paper made with
100% post consumer waste, processed chlorine free, and old growth free.

For every 5,000 books printed, New Society saves the following resources:[1]

26	Trees
2,391	Pounds of Solid Waste
2,631	Gallons of Water
3,432	Kilowatt Hours of Electricity
4,347	Pounds of Greenhouse Gases
19	Pounds of HAPs, VOCs, and AOX Combined
7	Cubic Yards of Landfill Space

[1]Environmental benefits are calculated based on research done by the Environmental Defense Fund and
other members of the Paper Task Force who study the environmental impacts of the paper industry.

For a full list of NSP's titles, please call **1-800-567-6772** *or check out our web site at:*

www.newsociety.com

NEW SOCIETY PUBLISHERS